The Work
Is Thine,
O Christ

The Work Is Thine, O Christ

In honor of
Erland Waltner

June Alliman Yoder
Editor

Institute of Mennonite Studies
2002

Published by Institute of Mennonite Studies, 3003 Benham Avenue, Elkhart IN 47517-1999

©2002 by Institute of Mennonite Studies

Printed in the United States of America by Evangel Press, Nappanee, Indiana

ISBN 0-936273-33-X

Library of Congress Cataloging-in-Publication Data

The work is thine, O Christ : in honor of Erland Waltner / edited by
June Alliman Yoder.
    p. cm.
  ISBN 0-936273-33-X (alk. paper)
  1. Waltner, Erland, 1914–. 2. Mennonites—Doctrines.
3. Mennonites—Sermons. 4. Sermons, American. I. Waltner, Erland, 1914–.
II. Yoder, June Alliman.
  BX8143.W25 W67 2002
  289.7'092—dc21

                         2002015725

Cover design by Mary E. Klassen.

Front cover photo by Mary E. Klassen.
Other photos courtesy of the Waltner family and the Associated Mennonite Biblical
Seminary photo files.

We are but links in a chain
that is being forged in a Hand
that is not our own,
involved in tasks
so overwhelming
that none of us
would choose them
for ourselves.

Erland Waltner
Mennonite Biblical Seminary inaugural address
October 1958

Contents

Foreword

I f Erland Waltner had been an architect, he would have built bridges. With his keen mind, careful planning, and extraordinary relational skills, he would have mobilized people and resources to span chasms that others thought impossible to cross.

Instead, God called Erland Waltner to build bridges of trust and faith as a pastor, theologian, professor, administrator, church statesman, scholar, and mentor. For more than six decades he has brought people together for the sake of the gospel—serving as bridge builder and strategist for what became Associated Mennonite Biblical Seminary, playing a pivotal role in building trust between the two largest Mennonite denominations in North America, and giving leadership to Mennonite World Conference.

Because the church of every generation is vulnerable to faction, we do well to reflect on what made this leader so effective in fostering unity in the church. The following were hallmarks of Erland's leadership:

Respect for others. Always ready to give the benefit of the doubt to opponents, and keen to identify some area of common ground, Erland conveys respect for others in a way that brings out the best in each.

Careful listening. Usually not the first to speak, and not one to dominate conversation, Erland builds trust by letting others know he cares how they feel and tries to understand what they are saying.

Strong confessional and biblical moorings. Erland persistently advanced the idea of putting *biblical* in the name of AMBS; he steadfastly proclaimed Jesus as Lord. By calling God's people to wrestle with Scripture and to follow Jesus, Erland has helped the church look beyond itself to what is truly life-giving.

Patience to work for change. A self-described gradualist, Erland has a long view of change in the church. When the church must reach across a great span of differences, he says, "you inch your way toward each other; you do not do it all at once." Erland not only survived decades in leadership, but managed institutions with a steady hand and calm spirit that allowed them to thrive.

Undaunted courage. Whether bringing together opponents in the fundamentalist-modernist debate, or working with Harold Bender to rebuild trust and communication among European Mennonites after grievous events of World War II, Erland took risks to attempt what others thought could not be done.

Vibrant personal piety. In recent years Erland has served as spiritual director to many, sharing rich insights from a lifetime of prayer, meditation, and waiting on God. Worship and involvement in a congregation have been foundational to his long ministry.

Because these patterns of leadership have inspired generations of students and faculty at AMBS, it is fitting that the seminary community name our main classroom and administrative building Waltner Hall. Erland was based in this building for almost half a century, variously leading the seminary, lecturing in the classroom, encouraging students, writing a commentary, and otherwise serving the church.

Thank you, Erland, for a lifetime of imaginative and faithful bridge building for the kingdom of God. The seminary and the church honor you with this collection of essays, with gratitude that you brought us closer to God and to one another.

J. Nelson Kraybill

President, Associated Mennonite Biblical Seminary

Preface

This book is about Erland Waltner. The whole book is about him. Even the parts that seem to be about ethics or aging or discipleship or 1 Peter or seminary education or spirituality are about Erland.

The first section of the book is a series of biographical essays that look at different periods of Erland's life. Five authors trace the issues, events, and people that shaped him from the early years to the present. As we read we watch Erland change in some ways, and in other ways we see him remain the same—servant of God, peacemaker, and thoughtful student of the Word.

The second section of the book is a collection of some of Erland's writings and addresses. These are arranged in chronological order so we can witness how they reflect his life journey both in content and in style. In this section we learn to know Erland by reading his own words written over the course of decades.

The third section of the book reflects the influence of Erland Waltner the professor. According to Erland, he was more at home in the classroom than in the boardroom. He taught with the authority of one who knows his subject matter, with the warmth and good humor of one who loves his students, and with the passion of one who believes deeply in the Jesus of the New Testament. As a Bible professor and a teacher of preaching, he comes to us as we hear his students proclaiming the Word of God. The power of mentors and teachers lies not in their capacity to turn out people who are just like themselves. Rather their influence is in their capacity to awaken a truth in us that helps us become more fully ourselves. So it is with Erland Waltner. The variety of voices, the breadth of concerns, and the many texts stand as a testimony to his influence as a teacher. Erland says he has preached more than four thousand sermons himself. Think of the number preached by his students. His influence is great, and his students' love for him is great. Every person I invited to contribute a sermon in honor of their former professor responded quickly and with enthusiasm.

The final section contains only one essay. I asked Erland Waltner to write a piece for this book, and when I read it I knew it needed to be the last word. In it he reflects on the hymn-prayer that has guided his life and labor: "The work is thine, O Christ." And a good work it has been, as we have seen it unfold in you, Erland.

This project was accomplished with deep satisfaction and great joy; however, the most ever-present emotion was gratitude. My gratitude to Erland Waltner for all that he has been for me is almost too great for words. He was a grand mentor to a fledgling teacher. He taught the gracious hospitality of the classroom as well as the elevated respect for the preached Word and public address. Indeed I feel I have been a student of the "obedient learner and obedient messenger," my dear brother and friend, Erland Waltner. I am grateful, Erland, for your willingness to allow us this window into your life which inspires us to live ours more faithfully.

The administrative cabinet of Associated Mennonite Biblical Seminary gave permission for this project to move ahead. The Waltner celebration committee, chaired by Mark Weidner, helped shape the book and guided the project to its completion. I am grateful for the trust of both of these groups.

To Institute of Mennonite Studies director Mary Schertz and the IMS executive committee: Thank you for your willingness to add this book to an already busy schedule. Your readiness to make room for this project was a gesture of support, and I found your encouragement and advice energizing.

Barbara Nelson Gingerich was an able managing editor in more ways than she may have wished. I came to rely on her judgment and her ability to juggle several projects at once. She knew when to challenge me and when to encourage me and did both in the right proportions. Amy Vachon worked as an editorial assistant. I am grateful to her for her passion for this project and her helpful research skills. Mary Klassen served as designer and photo editor for the book. Her experience, expertise, and gentle advice were deeply appreciated.

I also want to offer a word of gratitude to all the writers who took the time to be a part of this project. The book exists because of your efforts. I am grateful for your love for Erland Waltner and your enthusiasm for this project. You were all a joy to work with. Many of you are seasoned writers and editors, and I greatly appreciated your encouragement to me.

I conclude with gratitude to John, my editor-in-residence, who graciously read the manuscript and advised me along the way.

With gratitude to you all and to God.

JUNE ALLIMAN YODER

Erland Waltner:
His Life

I bear testimony
to the amazing grace of God
in my own life.
It is God's holy love
which has humbled and encouraged me…
Further I would recognize
my deep indebtedness
to all who have gone before me
in the love of the church
and in the life of the seminary.

Erland Waltner
Mennonite Biblical Seminary inaugural address
October 1958

1 | *Preparation of a leader*
Erland Waltner from Dakota to Elkhart

JAMES C. JUHNKE

ERLAND WALTNER HAS ALWAYS HAD A STRONG SENSE of heritage and of the hand of God in history.[1] In the opening words of his 1958 inaugural address as president of Mennonite Biblical Seminary, Erland spoke of "my deep indebtedness to all who have gone before me in the love of the church and in the life of the seminary.... We are but links in a chain which is being forged in a Hand that is not our own, involved in tasks so overwhelming that none of us would choose them for ourselves."[2]

Erland's love of the church originated in his home community of Freeman, South Dakota. Throughout his life, he has maintained close ties with home, communicating regularly with his parents, Benjamin and Emma Miller Waltner, who lived into their nineties, and also with siblings and friends in South Dakota after his parents' death.

For Erland, the known links of Waltner family lineage went back to a Hutterite community in the early eighteenth century in central Europe.[3] The line included strong leaders. George ("Jerg") Waldner, Erland's five-times great grandfather, was a teacher who left the Lutheran state church

---

James C. Juhnke is retired professor of history at Bethel College, North Newton, Kansas. As a student at Bethel, he took courses from Erland Waltner. He reports that one on Acts and the early church was "especially memorable for me. Decades later I drew on it when Harold Moyer and I collaborated on a musical drama based on Acts, 'Time Will Tell.'"

[1] This paper is based substantially on a series of tape-recorded and transcribed interviews I conducted with Erland Waltner in July 2000, in Elkhart, Indiana. The interview project was sponsored by Institute for Mennonite Studies. Copies of the unedited transcripts are available at the IMS office at Associated Mennonite Biblical Seminary and at Bethel College in Kansas. Most of Erland Waltner's collected papers are at Mennonite Library and Archives at Bethel College, but have not yet been processed and indexed for research.

[2] "Education for Apostleship," Inaugural Address, Mennonite Biblical Seminary, October 26, 1958. The address appears in this book on pages 59–67.

[3] On the history of the Waltner family, see Gary J. Waltner, *The Joseph Waltner Family, Tracing the Second Son of Andreas and Katharina Schrag Waldner of the Bruderhof Raditschewa, Russia, 1797–1960* (Freeman, S.D., 1962).

and joined the Hutterites. George's son, Johannes Waldner (1749–1824), also a teacher, became one of the Hutterite leaders. Johannes made several trips to St. Petersburg to advocate before the Russian authorities in behalf of the interests of his people. He was also one of the authors of the *Klein Geschichtsbuch*, a volume that chronicled the life of the Hutterite people. One of Johannes' sons, Andreas (b. 1777), married a Katharina Schrag, whose people had migrated from Bern Canton in Switzerland to the Palatinate and then to eastern Europe. Katharina's people, who came to be known as Swiss-Volhynians, followed the Amish discipline, but shifted from Amish to Mennonite identity during the years surrounding their migration to the United States. So Erland Waltner has Hutterite, Amish, and Mennonite roots.

Erland Waltner grew up on the fringe of the Mennonite settlement of Freeman, South Dakota. He became keenly aware of ethnic-national diversity among different Mennonite ethnic groups as well as among different kinds of Americans. The farms of his father (Benjamin J. Waltner) and his uncles (Ed, Emil, John, and Henry) were located about twelve miles southeast of the town of Freeman in what was known as Spring Valley. To the west of Freeman lived the Hutters—people of Hutterite background who migrated at the same time. To the north were the Low German Mennonites, who originated in the Dutch and North German wing of the Anabaptist movement and who spoke a different German dialect. Despite their ethnic differences, these three groups (Swiss, Hutters, and Low Germans) cooperated in community and educational matters, most notably in the founding of Freeman Academy in 1903.

Erland was seven years old when he first attended public school in district #38, where non-Mennonites (mostly Lutherans of Danish, Norwegian, and German background) were the majority. But his parents, Benjamin and Emma Miller Waltner, neither of whom had attended school beyond the eighth grade, had already taught him reading, writing, and arithmetic at home. Benjamin Waltner was a man of great intellectual curiosity. He read books and magazines, systematically collected scientific information about plant and animal life, and kept careful financial records in a family journal. Father was in charge of discipline, or, as Erland puts it, "Dad was the law and Mom was the gospel, but they got along quite well." Dad also led the family devotions each morning, reading from the German Bible. The family all knelt for prayer, facing the backs of their chairs, a practice of piety typical among Swiss-Volhynian Mennonites.

One of Erland's earliest childhood memories dates from 1919 when he was four years old. His uncle Ed Waltner returned home from military prison after World War I. Uncle Ed had refused the military uniform and training and had been court-martialed and imprisoned at Fort Leavenworth. What did it mean to belong to a people whose religious pacifist convictions might require going to prison? Erland embarked early on the path that led to seminary and graduate school theses on questions of church and state, war and peace.

In public school as well as in the Salem Mennonite Church (the "south church"), Erland had strong Mennonite teachers who inspired him toward leadership. One was John D. Unruh, principal of Marion High School where Erland attended. At the Salem church, William S. Gottshall was the pastor who instructed and baptized Erland when he was fifteen and made a decision for Christ and the church. Erland responded positively to Gottshall's warm pastoral style, his commitment to personal Bible reading, and his teaching that we are all sinners who need Christ as Savior and Lord.

The church was intentional in calling Erland to leadership. When Erland spoke at a Sunday school convention in Henderson, Nebraska, P. A. Penner, missionary on furlough from India, challenged him to consider going into "full-time Christian service." On one occasion the deacons of the Salem congregation made a visit to the Waltner home to talk with Erland and his parents about his future.

Peter R. Schroeder, who was pastor of the Salem church when Erland was ready for college, was an outspoken anti-modernist. Both Gottshall and Schroeder were critical of alleged liberal tendencies at Bethel College and Bluffton College. When Erland left for Bethel after a year at Freeman Junior College, Schroeder took him aside and said, "Now when you go to Bethel College, you be a discerning person. Be careful, there will be some teachers there that you will not want to go along with."[4] As Erland remembers, his home congregation was "at least eighty percent inclined towards a fundamentalist position." More critical of fundamentalism were his uncle Emil Waltner, a professor at Yankton College, and his aunt Lena Waltner, who later taught art at Bethel College.

So Erland went to Bethel College with his guard up. In letters to his parents, he wrote that he was part of a conservative minority that was working and praying for spiritual renewal on campus. In the fall of his first semester, he presented his first church sermon as part of a gospel team at a Sunday evening meeting at the Alexanderwohl Mennonite congregation. It was the first of Erland's more than four thousand sermons, and the topic was "Jesus and Sinners." He also honed his

---

[4] Erland Waltner interview, July 16, 2000, p. 16.

speaking skills as a member of the debate team. In his junior year, his team won all five of their debates at the national debate tournament in Lexington, Kentucky.

Among Erland's influential Bible teachers at Bethel were Abraham Warkentin and H. W. Lohrentz. Warkentin later became the first president of Mennonite Biblical Seminary in Chicago. Lohrentz, president of Tabor College, introduced his students to historical critical study in a balanced and moderate way. Erland found something lacking in the evolution-based science classes at Bethel. In the summer of 1934, between his junior and senior years, he went to Wheaton College for courses on theism and evolution, which provided a more solid theistic foundation. Two of the more liberal teachers at Bethel who influenced Erland were Emmet L. Harshbarger and Edmund G. Kaufman. Harshbarger, a history teacher for whom Erland worked as student assistant, introduced him to the value of historical cultures and to the deeper social and political dimensions of Mennonite peace witness. Harshbarger strongly encouraged him to go on to graduate study in history. Kaufman, the college president, taught a course in comparative religions. Erland argued with him often. Kaufman encouraged Erland to attend seminary and helped him get a scholarship to Biblical Seminary in New York (BSNY). Walter Gering, a respected Freeman lad who had studied in New York and returned to pastor the town church, Bethany Mennonite, also influenced Erland in the direction of BSNY.

Erland did not necessarily consider the move to BSNY in 1935 vocationally definitive. Until 1937 he kept open the possibility of a career as a college teacher of history. For two summers, after graduation from Bethel and after his first year at seminary, Erland took graduate courses in history at the University of South Dakota. One brilliant history professor there, Dr. Herbert Shell, was an open atheist who scorned Christian belief. Erland was not intimidated by a professor who in some ways contradicted his values. He had long since learned that Mennonites were on the margins of the dominant culture. He sensed that the honest quest for historical truth could strengthen Mennonite identity and mission. He maintained this historical interest and consciousness even after he decided on the seminary track and a future in church ministry.

Biblical Seminary in New York, located in downtown Manhattan (235 East 49th Street), was a nondenominational school, founded by Wilbert Webster White (1863–1944).[5] The seminary, seen as more conservative than some other schools that upcoming Mennonite leaders

---

[5] Steve Nolt, "An Evangelical Encounter: Mennonites and the Biblical Seminary in New York," *Mennonite Quarterly Review* 70 (October 1996): 389–417.

attended, was known for its "Biblio-centric program" and a strong emphasis on missions. BSNY bypassed the divisive issues raised by historical literary criticism by elevating the role of inductive Bible study. The faculty viewed higher criticism as a useful tool, not to be dogmatically rejected as in more fundamentalist Bible schools. But the primary focus at BSNY was on careful examination and listening to the original text, in Greek or Hebrew if possible, but certainly in the vernacular. The idea, according to Erland, who now struggles with macular degeneration, was that the student should be so familiar with the biblical text "that you know it as well as your own home. If you were blind, you could still find your way around."

Erland thrived at BSNY. His practical ministries assignment was with a mission in Lower East Side Manhattan, a multi-ethnic area where he had startling encounters with the seamy side of urban life. Among Erland's most influential teachers were Howard Tillman Kuist, Donald G. Miller, and Dean Greer McKee. There were three excellent women teachers: Emily Werner, Dr. Carolyn Palmer, and Professor Woods. Edwin Lewis, a visiting professor from Drew University, introduced Erland to the theology of Karl Barth. Erland especially appreciated Barth's emphasis on the self-revealing nature of God, the centrality of Christ, and the role of Scripture. Another important guest professor was Julius Richter from the University of Berlin, professor of missiology. Richter was deeply troubled by the rise of Adolf Hitler and the course of political events in Germany.

For his bachelor of sacred theology thesis at BSNY, Erland wrote a 165-page study of "The Development of the Doctrine of Church and State in Anabaptism." He presented Anabaptism as a religious movement, not a social revolution. "In their vision of religious liberty and in their pleas for the moral purity of the church they were centuries ahead of their time." Erland portrayed Menno Simons as a broad-minded and practical reformer who offered a moderate and middle way between the extremes of Hutterite separation and Münsterite apocalypticism. The Anabaptist way had special relevance in 1938 when "the precious possession of religious liberty and the autonomy of the Church is again endangered by the rising tide of State totalitarianism."[6]

In the summer after graduation, Erland and a graduate student friend, Howard Hopper, traveled to the Holy Land and Europe. They learned firsthand about the looming crisis in Germany and the varying responses of German Mennonite leaders to it. Benjamin Unruh,

---

[6] Erland Waltner, "The Development of the Doctrine of Church and State in Anabaptism" (bachelor's thesis, Biblical Seminary in New York, 1938), 147–8.

Mennonite professor, had a life-size portrait of Adolf Hitler in his home. Christian Neff of Weierhof wept as he told of Mennonite youth being attracted to National Socialism. In Berlin, Erland and Howard met with a Jewish friend who had been at BSNY and now dramatically reported on the persecution faced by Jews in Germany. The 1938 trip was a boost to Erland's international awareness.

While at seminary, Erland and four or five other students formed what they called the Cautious Club in a common professed commitment not to get too involved with women. To his father, Erland wrote, "Dad, you know, the girls are getting along well without me and I'm getting along fairly well without them. Anyway, it costs so much, now, to date." On the volleyball court during his senior year, Erland and Winifred Schlosser went after the same ball and bumped heads—hard. Winifred fainted. When she recovered consciousness, Erland apologized and arranged for their first date. He remained a faithful Cautious Club member, however, until returning from his trip to Europe. Erland and Winifred were engaged in September 1938 and married in June 1939 in Greenville, Illinois, at Greenville College, the Free Methodist school where Winifred had graduated. Winifred had completed a masters of religious education degree at BSNY.

Erland had dated many Mennonite girls along the way, so it was a shock to his family that he would marry someone not a Mennonite. Two things made the adjustment easier. By remarkable coincidence, Winifred was the granddaughter of a Schlosser family who had lived in South Dakota on a farm between Freeman and Marion, about ten miles from the Waltner home. The Mennonites knew about the Schlosser school where Winifred's father, George Schlosser, had been a teacher. Moreover, George Schlosser, after a disillusioning tour of military duty in the Spanish-American War, renounced militarism and became a missionary, first in Africa and then in China where he married Mary Ogren. Mary, who was also a missionary in China, first learned to know George while both were studying at Greenville College in Illinois. Winifred was born and raised in China. Her free Methodist piety with its holiness emphasis was more expressive than the reserved piety of Erland's people. Both Erland and Winifred hoped the other would convert. As it turned out, Winifred made the greater adjustments, but together they made a fine blend. To the union were born four daughters: Mary Frances (1941), Winifred Irene ("Renie," 1946), Joy Kathleen, ("Kathy," 1949) and Rose Elaine (1953).

Erland's first pastorate after graduating from seminary was at Second Mennonite Church in Philadelphia. Another option would have been Downey Mennonite Church in Los Angeles, California, but Erland wanted to be near Winifred, who was working at a camp in New Jersey. Also, he wanted to continue his seminary education. His three years (1938–41) in Philadelphia were remarkably busy and productive. In addition to his full-time pastorate, Erland took some classes at Princeton Theological Seminary and enrolled at Eastern Baptist Seminary, where he wrote a master of theology thesis on the theology of Reinhold Niebuhr and completed the course work for a doctor of theology degree.

Second Mennonite Church of Philadelphia was a congregation of about a hundred members, a former mission outpost of First Mennonite Church. They had had only one pastor, Silas Grubb, who had been there for thirty-eight years. Erland's ministry resulted in more young people attending the church. The urban situation was light-years removed from rural South Dakota, both in the social problems faced by young people and on occasions such as a Sunday evening service when a stranger walked in from the street and pushed Erland aside with the words, "I have a word from the Lord to speak to this congregation."

For his master of theology thesis, Erland wrote on the influence of Karl Barth on the theology of Reinhold Niebuhr.[7] William Mueller, a German Baptist pacifist, advised the project. The thesis allowed Erland to delve more deeply into the theological question of human sin. Niebuhr, the most prominent American theologian of the time, had been an idealistic pacifist but in the 1930s had shifted from an idealistic to a realistic conception of human nature. Erland's thesis was descriptive. He did not attempt to engage Niebuhr's theology from an Anabaptist perspective. But it is clear that Erland was searching for a theological framework that would enable Mennonites to affirm the historic Anabaptist peace witness in a modern context while taking account of the depths of human sinfulness so evident in the world situation and so forcefully presented by Niebuhr.

In 1940, P. R. Schroeder, then pastor of Bethel Mennonite Church in Mountain Lake, Minnesota, was dying of cancer and recommended that the congregation call Erland Waltner to replace him. Moved by the endorsement from his own former pastor, Erland accepted the invitation. Missionary P. A. Penner, who years earlier had challenged Erland to full-time Christian service, installed him as pastor. The Waltner family arrived in Mountain Lake on December 7, 1941, the day of the Japanese attack on Pearl Harbor. The challenges of the war and the postwar era defined Erland's ministry in Mountain Lake, 1941–49. The congregation's

---

[7] Erland Waltner, "Evidences of Barthian Anthropology in the Theological Writings of Reinhold Niebuhr" (master's thesis, Eastern Baptist Theological Seminary, 1940).

history book labels this period as "Battle with Our Conscience."[8] The Bethel church was the largest congregation in a small town, and it had attracted members who were not inclined to the historic Mennonite peace position. It was a time of rapid changes, including the final shift from use of German to English language, the abandonment of the ceremony of footwashing, and the introduction of a young people's fellowship.

Bethel was a growing congregation, located near a Mennonite hospital and nurses home. The congregation was just completing a new church building when Erland arrived. Between fifty and sixty young men from the congregation were drafted or volunteered for alternative service as conscientious objectors or for military service in the United States armed forces—about half in each direction. There was an American flag in the church sanctuary. Erland was firmly committed to the historic Mennonite position of refusal of military service. He made pastoral visits to men in Civilian Public Service camps, but his ministry also embraced families with young men in military service. One issue was how to conduct funerals for men from the congregation who died in the war. Erland insisted that veterans not bring weapons into the church building, but compromised on the issue of a military salute at the grave site. The family decided whether an American flag should cover the casket.

The Bethel church had long had a distinguished record of producing missionaries, pastors, and leaders for the wider church. This continued under Erland's pastoral leadership. One wartime volunteer, Marie K. Fast, was assigned by Mennonite Central Committee to the United Nations Relief and Rehabilitation Administration and lost her life in 1945 when her ship went down in the Adriatic Sea. During the war, four members of the congregation were ordained to the ministry.

Erland was in demand for leadership elsewhere in the denomination. Abraham Warkentin, Erland's Bible teacher from Bethel and president of Mennonite Biblical Seminary (MBS) in Chicago, invited him to join the MBS faculty. In 1947, Erland commuted from Mountain Lake to Chicago to teach a class in the MBS Bible School. During his ministry in Mountain Lake, Erland continued to work on his Th.D. thesis at Eastern Baptist. That thesis flowed naturally from his earlier work on Anabaptism, church and state, and Niebuhrian theology, but moved toward biblical study. The title was "An Analysis of the Mennonite Views on the Christian's Relation to the State in the Light of the New Testament." Without directly attacking Niebuhr, Erland affirmed Menno

---

[8] Aganetha Loewen, *The Story of Bethel Mennonite Church* (Mountain Lake, 1990), 12–19.

Simons' position that Christian rulers could "conduct their functions according to the principles of Christ." New Testament teachings did not forbid participating in the political order and holding political office, but the primary task of the church was spiritual. Indeed, Erland wrote, "General Conference Mennonites need a new emphasis upon evangelism without which the efforts to legislate moral reform or to preserve world peace are futile."[9]

Although Erland had been critical of Bethel College and its president, E. G. Kaufman, he responded positively in 1949 to the invitation to teach Bible at Bethel. Kaufman courted him with the line, "Well, Bethel is not the way it should be, but come help us make it better." During his eight years of teaching at Bethel (1949–57), Erland strengthened the offerings of the Bible department and increased enrollment in Bible classes. He taught the course for entering freshmen, "The Life of Christ," to hundreds of students. Later he taught the capstone course required of all seniors, "Basic Christian Convictions," which had long been taught by the president.

Among the contentious issues, vigorously debated in the Mennonite press at the time, was which translation of the Bible to use. Erland preferred the Revised Standard Version, but allowed students to choose a different version. His tenure at Bethel included many opportunities for preaching and for leading Bible studies in the churches.

Early in his time at Bethel, leaders of Grace Bible Institute in Omaha, Nebraska, contacted him about becoming president of that institution. Among the interesting "What if?" questions of Mennonite history is how Grace Bible Institute might have developed under Erland's leadership, with his strong commitment to Anabaptism, biblical pacifism, and a Christocentric interpretation of Scripture. At Grace Bible Institute, Erland would have been less likely to have students like one at Bethel, a declared nonbeliever who wrote on his examination, "I don't believe this stuff, but these are the answers you want." (Erland gave the student an "A" for in fact knowing what the teacher wanted!) The invitation from Grace demonstrated that Erland had gained the confidence of both the liberal and conservative wings of the denomination. That centering leadership helped him at Bethel College as well as later at Mennonite Biblical Seminary.

Erland's preparation for leadership included trips to Europe in the summers of 1949 (with Harold Bender and Cornelius Rempel) and 1951 to evaluate Mennonite Central Committee programs there and to

---

[9] Erland Waltner, "An Analysis of the Mennonite Views on the Christian's Relation to the State in the Light of the New Testament" (Th.D. diss., Eastern Baptist Theological Seminary, 1948).

provide pastoral services. In 1956, he was elected president of the General Conference Mennonite Church, a position he held until 1962. In the summer of 1956, the conference decided to move Mennonite Biblical Seminary from Chicago to Elkhart, Indiana, with a view to increasing cooperation with the (Old) Mennonite Church and its seminary at Goshen. The decision was vigorously opposed by E. G. Kaufman and Lloyd Ramseyer of Bethel and Bluffton Colleges. Ever since his graduate school days, Erland had appreciated his contacts with Harold Bender and others at Goshen. In the summer of 1954, while he was still on the faculty at Bethel, Erland taught a course on the Petrine Epistles for a joint Mennonite Biblical Seminary and Goshen Biblical Seminary session held at Goshen. The contacts made and confidence built at that time served him well in future seminary relationships.

Erland was a member of the MBS board at the time of the decision to move to Elkhart. At an earlier point, he would have favored a move from Chicago to join the Goshen Biblical Seminary in Goshen, but many General Conference leaders opposed that idea. His possible move to the seminary had been discussed for some time. The decision came after the 1956 General Conference meeting. In his final year of teaching at Bethel, 1956–57, he was also planning for the establishment of a new MBS campus at Elkhart.

The summer of 1957 was a busy time for Erland and Winifred Waltner and their four daughters, ages four though sixteen. While Cornelius Miller was rushing to build a new house for them in the recently purchased seminary property of farm fields south of Elkhart, Erland and Winifred went to attend the Mennonite World Conference assembly in Karlsruhe, West Germany. Upon their return the family moved from North Newton to Elkhart. The groundbreaking for the new seminary buildings was in September of that year.

It was a time of new beginnings. All of Erland Waltner's life experiences, from his youth in South Dakota to his tenure as Bible professor at Bethel College, had prepared him for this new challenge of denominational leadership.

2 | *President of Mennonite Biblical Seminary*

CORNELIUS J. DYCK

A GROUND-BREAKING CEREMONY FOR MENNONITE Biblical Seminary (MBS) had been held on September 3, 1957, on fifty-five acres of farmland on the south edge of Elkhart. By the fall of 1958, Henry Knuck, an outstanding builder originally from the Netherlands, had constructed a U-shaped building for a library, classrooms, and administrative offices, as well as several student housing units. Library books, pianos, and all other moveable furniture had been brought from 4614 Woodlawn Avenue in south Chicago to the new Elkhart location, facilitated by the newly completed Indiana toll road. The new president, Erland Waltner, had built a house for his family next to the campus, making it an instant landmark by painting it red. Fifty-eight students had arrived, and classes had begun as scheduled. Everything had gone well!

Actually, not quite. A labor union representing construction workers had publicly expressed its anger at builder Knuck for not employing union workers. Members set up picket lines at campus entrances, which some building materials suppliers refused to cross. The picketers themselves were friendly. Faculty and others enjoyed visiting with them. They reassured the seminary that they had no problem with the new school. Knuck, however, apparently had had earlier encounters with the union and decided this was the time and the project to fight it. He knew he was paying higher than union wages, and that the Elkhart community favored the seminary's coming. And this was a church-related project! Despite the best efforts of Harry Martens, assistant to the seminary president and a skilled mediator, the case ended up in court. The union lost and an elated Knuck could proceed with construction. While the seminary was glad to see the work continue, it was troubled at having been the cause of this episode and did not quite know how to cope with it. It also led to intense discussions in class sessions the

---

Cornelius J. Dyck is professor emeritus of Anabaptist and sixteenth century studies at Associated Mennonite Biblical Seminary, Elkhart, Indiana.

following year: labor unions and Mennonites, an immediate case study. But the faculty may have been too new on location to know just what to do with what had happened, beyond discussions in class and over coffee.

Why Elkhart? If MBS wanted to work with Goshen College Biblical Seminary (GCBS), why not move to Goshen? In fact, MBS had been invited to move to Goshen, but a good number of General Conference (GC) leaders, particularly those with roots in the "Old" Mennonite (MC) church, feared that the much larger MC group and college might swallow up the small MBS school, and it would lose its identity. Some district conferences and the GC colleges also had reservations. In 2002, these fears may seem quaint, with MCs and GCs having become (largely) one body, but they were real in the 1950s, rooted in issues of polity and authority (e.g., the power of the "bench"), the plain coat and prayer covering, and in general, a different counter-culture stance among MCs than the GCs were comfortable with.

Canadian GCs could not quite understand these undercurrents, possibly because, as immigrants from Russia, they lacked awareness of denominational dynamics in the U.S. Then too most MC congregations in Canada were in Ontario, with few in western Canada where the immigrants of the 1870s and 1920s had been officially encouraged to settle. Except for Civilian Public Service (CPS) and Mennonite Central Committee (MCC) work, and a few committee experiences, the two groups did not know each other well. Also, parts of Canadian GC polity may have been closer to MC history and practice. Consider, for example, the authority of elders and bishops such as David Toews, J. J. Thiesssen, J. H. Janzen, J. G. Rempel, and David Schulz.

As early as 1954, Erland Waltner suggested Elkhart as a compromise location. That summer he also taught a course on the Petrine Epistles at GCBS and had as his students Canadians Peter Wiebe, William Klassen, David Schroeder, and Peter J. Dyck. S. F. Pannabecker writes: "From informal contacts in a joint summer school session with Goshen College Biblical Seminary in 1954, there came a suggestion for a serious study of an inter-Mennonite effort at ministerial training. Proposals were made which eventually received official consideration, and after several revisions, a plan of cooperation between MBS and GCBS was approved and embodied in a formal memorandum of agreement.[1] But even two years earlier in 1952, according to Peter J.

---

[1] Samuel Floyd Pannabecker, *Open Doors: The History of the General Conference Mennonite Church* (Newton: Faith and Life Pr., 1975), 372. The memorandum of agreement went into effect August 1, 1958. It was drafted and approved by the Joint Coordinating Committee, consisting of Paul Mininger, president of Goshen College and Goshen College Biblical

Dyck, who was studying at GCBS, Waltner and GCBS dean Harold S. Bender had talked about the possibility of the two seminaries coming together, which led to each inviting four friends to the Bender home one evening for "Anabaptist tea" and to discuss this issue. No decisions were made, but it was one step in a series of steps, which ultimately led to MBS moving to the south side of Elkhart in 1958 and cooperation with GCBS.[2]

INAUGURATION

On Sunday afternoon, October 26, 1958, at 2:30, a "Service of Inauguration for Erland Waltner As President of Mennonite Biblical Seminary" was held in Elkhart at the Church of the Brethren, Wolf and Benham Avenues. It was a formal and impressive service, with Arthur S. Rosenberger, chairman of the MBS board, presiding. The members of the board were, in addition to Rosenberger, Jesse N. Smucker, Raymond L. Hartzler, Elmer Baumgartner, Willard Claassen, J. Herbert Fretz, Amos E. Kreider, John Wichert, and Olin A. Krehbiel. Also present were Arnold Nickel and William E. Keeney (alumni), E. G. Kaufman (Bethel), Lloyd L. Ramseyer (Bluffton), John K. Ewert (Freeman), I. I. Friesen (Canadian Mennonite Bible College), and representatives of eleven other theological schools.

The service opened with the processional hymn "Joyful, joyful, we adore thee"; the invocation by Robert W. Hartzler, Goshen pastor; and the Scripture lesson read by I. I. Friesen, CMBC president and vice president of the General Conference. The seminary choir, under the direction of Marvin Dirks, sang "Send out thy light," and R. L. Hartzler led in the service of induction and prayer of inauguration. Then Arthur S. Rosenberger, chairman of the board and pastor of West Swamp Mennonite Church in Quakertown, Pennsylvania, gave the following charge to the candidate, quoted in full here for historical purposes and to help us reflect on the nature of the seminary presidency at that time:

In view of the call of the Board of Trustees to you, Erland Waltner, to become the president of Mennonite Biblical Seminary, and in view of your acceptance

Seminary; Harold S. Bender, dean of GCBS; Erland Waltner, president of MBS; and S. F. Pannabecker, dean of MBS. The memorandum goes into amazing detail. It provides for committees and organizational responsibility, but also includes the clause: "This agreement shall not be considered to be a legal contract, but as the brotherly and Christian equivalent to the same..." (article 8, no. 4). The document breathes caution. In *Open Doors,* Pannabecker writes that objection to locating "on or near the Goshen College campus... almost broke up the negotiations" (ibid., 373).

[2] Peter J. Dyck, "Drinking Anabaptist Tea and Other Tales of Integration," in *Gathering at the Hearth,* ed. John E. Sharp (Scottdale: Herald Pr., 2001), 199–202.

of this call, I hereby formally, in this inauguration ceremony, declare you to be installed in this office. As you have been called with the conviction of the board that this is God's leading and since you have responded with the assurance that to accept the call is his will for you, this installation is carried out with the prayer that God may richly bless you and use you as the President of Mennonite Biblical Seminary.

Ye did not choose me, but I chose you, and appointed you, that ye should go and bear fruit, and that your fruit should abide. John 15:16

The Board of Trustees and the friends of this institution are of the conviction that God has chosen and appointed you, Erland Waltner, to be our president. We are also of the conviction that God has chosen Mennonite Biblical Seminary to have a real place in the work of his kingdom.

During the time that I have served on this board I and my fellow board members have experienced many evidences of God's leading. We have had to make many decisions and take forward steps on faith. We sought always to ascertain God's will and he has led us to this point in a remarkable way.

You, Erland Waltner, are the third president of Mennonite Biblical Seminary. The choice of each man for this office was tied up with special circumstances. Dr. A. Warkentin was our first president. During the summer of 1945 we felt very definitely the leading of God that it was time to get started with the program of Mennonite Biblical Seminary. So venturing out on faith, we set a number of conditions whereby we might be assured to go ahead. Among these were that we might have ten students, that an association with Bethany Biblical Seminary could be arranged, and that we would find a man to serve as president. All these worked out in our favor. We found Brother Warkentin available to serve as president and definitely feeling that the Lord had called him so to serve. We revere the memory of this man who served so faithfully till his death two years later.

The second president of our institution was Floyd Pannabecker. When the board called Brother Pannabecker to serve on our staff he was in China doing relief work. A cablegram was sent asking him to be the dean of our institution. When the answer came in the affirmative we definitely felt again that God had appointed another man to a vital place of leadership in the school. As Dr. Warkentin became ill then passed away, Floyd Pannabecker served as acting president and then became president. God has used him in a large way in the service of our institution and the church in general.

Upon the request of Brother Pannabecker to be relieved of the duties of the office of president, the board again, with prayer and seeking the will of God, sought for his successor and we turned to you, Brother Waltner. Having come to the conviction that the time had come to think in terms of an associated Mennonite relationship in our seminary work, you took our call under consideration with the provision that we work with you to explore the possibilities of such an associated relationship. As we did this we found the brethren of other Mennonite groups were also minded to make the same exploration and we entered into conferences looking toward this end. Thus under the leading of God for our day we came to the goal of the associated relationship which we all see as something tremendously significant and vitally important.

Now, Brother Waltner, the task that comes to you in the presidential office is among others that of leading us in our group on into the development and practical accomplishments of all that this association can mean. May you have the pleasure some day of working not only with the Goshen College Biblical Seminary but also with other groups of our Mennonite brotherhood as they may feel God's direction to them to enter into the association.

While from the standpoint of this highly significant new movement I have up to this point spoken of your continuing responsibility in the associated relationship, I would also now briefly call your attention to some other aspects of the charge that is given you today.

As president of our seminary you are still first of all a minister of the gospel of Jesus Christ. You continue to share with your brother ministers the prime responsibility of preaching Jesus Christ and his gospel, of witnessing for him, and of seeking to lead others into a right relationship to him and growing experience with him. You have had a large ministry in many churches and schools in this capacity, and as you assume and carry out your seminary duties, you are still appointed to be a good minister of Jesus Christ. May he bless you in that ministry right here in the seminary and also serve our constituency in your contacts with them.

Then also you are continuing to be a teacher as you direct and participate in the training of young people for Christian service. All our teachers have a high responsibility as the kind of young people who go out from such an institution as ours will have great bearing on what kind of a church we are. You have had large opportunities in this area. We continue to look to you to use your God given talents in providing the best type of constructive study as in Bible and related courses our future ministers, missionaries, and religious education teachers come under your instruction.

Again, you are challenged in this office with the administration of an institution. You are not unfamiliar with these duties but you will be wrestling with them in larger measure than ever before. The task of an administrator is never easy. Problems loom up on every side, decisions must constantly be made, and an aggressive forward looking constructive program must ever be kept in motion. Each of these phases can involve much. We are confident you can meet all of them with the help of God. May you have that insight and wisdom that is not only a tremendous asset but [also] a prime necessity for any administrator.

As you enter upon your duties with consecration, devotion, enthusiasm, and a sense of God's help, you will have a staff, a board of trustees, a constituency which to a large degree is of a mind to work with you in your great task. As you, as the one whom we are fully persuaded is chosen and appointed of God to lead us, are formally installed today in this office, we pledge our support and cooperation, and pray that the spirit of God may lead you to a large and fruitful career as the President of Mennonite Biblical Seminary.[3]

Following this address, given with great care and dignity, and the hymn "Pour out thy Spirit," Erland Waltner presented his inaugural address, entitled "Education for Apostleship," beginning with the humble admission that "We are but links in a chain which is being forged in a Hand that is not our own, involved in tasks so overwhelming that none of us would choose them for ourselves."[4] Speaking first to the question of why a seminary is needed, Waltner confesses that as a new administrator, this "must seem presumptive, ...yet is shared as vision and aspiration which requires the seasoning of experience." Then, in justifying his use of the term "apostleship" in relationship to the familiar term "discipleship," he states that "the disciple is in essence the obedient learner [while] the apostle is in essence the obedient messenger."

The context of education for apostleship is then spelled out in five polarities: (1) freedom and commitment, i.e., the concept of a community of learning which is also a community of faith; (2) scholarship and the spiritual life, i.e., the seminary as a community of rigorous and creative intellectual disciplines but also a community of warm and fertile spiritual nurture; (3) biblical studies and modern man, i.e., the seminary as a community of the Bible without minimizing the disciplines of human understanding; (4) content and communication, i.e., the seminary as a theological community as well as a witnessing community; and (5) denominationalism and ecumenism, i.e., the seminary as a community committed to ecclesiastical [denominational] loyalty as well as to ongoing Christian conversation with other traditions. These polarities are gathered up at the end under the rubric "A vision summarized," a clear statement of his plans for the seminary in the years ahead.[5]

---

[3] Waltner collection, AMBS archives. See also Samuel Floyd Pannabecker, *Ventures of Faith: The Story of Mennonite Biblical Seminary* (Elkhart: Mennonite Biblical Seminary, 1975).

[4] The address appears in this book on pages 59–67.

[5] Ibid., 67.

The address was followed by the hymn "The work is thine, O Christ" and the benediction given by J. E. Hartzler, former president of Witmarsum Theological Seminary.

CALLING A FACULTY

The new president had every intention of making the new Elkhart seminary an excellent one. For this he needed to recruit quality teachers who, preferably, had pastoral experience even as he had, and who were equally competent both in the classroom and in the churches of the constituency. Yet only three came from Chicago with the seminary: S. F. Pannabecker, who taught missions and American church history, while also serving as dean; Jacob Enz, who taught Old Testament and Hebrew; and Marvin Dirks in music and worship. William Klassen, fresh from Princeton, was added for New Testament. However, since the agreement specified that one-fourth of the courses be offered jointly, the GCBS faculty brought significant strength in H. S. Bender, J. Lawrence Burkholder, Howard Charles, Paul Miller, and John H. Yoder. I was added in historical theology in 1959. Adjunct faculty were employed as needed and new faculty and staff added, including Leland and Bertha Harder, later also Clarence Bauman in theology.

Changes were made in the curriculum, including requiring Greek and Hebrew in the three-year pastoral program, which GCBS already had. This greatly expanded the curricular time required by the Bible department, a fact the other two departments did not always appreciate, but Waltner certainly favored, though he himself taught courses in English Bible. He considered it important for administrators to know the classroom. During this period, the president and S. F. Pannabecker, dean of MBS, worked intensely at accreditation, which was received in 1964 with help from GCBS, which had already been accredited in 1958.

THE CHALLENGE OF THE '60S

Yet barely had the seminary and its president settled into a routine when the long overdue civil rights movement and the Vietnam war broke on the national scene. The impact on seminary students was almost immediate, beginning with the challenging of authority, any authority, soon including questions about the traditional pastoral ministry and church life itself. Seven out of fifteen students in their second year dropped out of the B.D. program at MBS in 1963. By the fall of 1964, the president reported "persisting problems" to the seminary board, specifically student questions about why a few were being trained as leaders instead of all the laity. As Pannabecker points out, this was really

a call to expand "a ministerial training school into a theological school."[6]
The president, dean, and faculty worked to this end, but enrollment
during the '60s was disappointing. Erland Waltner worked hard in the
churches during these years. The seminary was fortunate to have as
president a man whom the churches respected and trusted.

This confidence was also seen in the fact that Waltner was elected to
be president of the General Conference Mennonite Church from 1956
(Winnipeg) to 1962 (Bethlehem). Sometimes this office dealt with
problems he may have wished someone else would handle. Thus, at the
1959 (Bluffton) General Conference sessions, in a foretaste of the coming
'60s, a group that might be described as coming from the religious right
spoke against resolutions opposing capital punishment and developing
nuclear energy, and also opposed the work of the conference and
seminary on race relations. Efforts to talk in committee proved futile, and
the group introduced a resolution on the inspiration and inerrancy of the
Bible. When a seminary faculty member responded, although he was
probably misunderstood, the seminary still had a major public relations
challenge on its hands.

But the '60s were not nearly over and the president's plate kept
filling up. In 1962, Fred Carter, an African-American, asked to buy a lot
from the seminary to build a house. This caused immediate uproar
among white neighbors, including a cross burning on campus. But the
seminary was committed to open occupancy and invited the neighbors
to talk. They were upset. When one asked me whether I was a Christian,
and I answered, "Yes," the young man jumped up, grabbed me by the
shirt, saying, "No, you're not, you're a [expletive deleted] commie, and
I'm going to take you outside and show you how we treat commies."
Fortunately some of his friends calmed him and, as Pannabecker writes,
"Mr. Carter's house turned out to be a credit to the community and his
lawn the best kept on the street."[7]

In 1964, the seminary chapel was built. The architect had been
asked to include space for an organ, for which specifications had been
received. It took some years at the factory to build the organ. One day,
late in the 1960s, a large semi began unloading the Schlicker instrument
near the chapel. Students soon learned what was in the boxes. Some
were mildly concerned, and others were greatly disturbed. One letter,
signed by two men, urged that the money invested be spent for the poor:
"The organ is one more mistake among a whole host of mistakes
Christians are making.... [It is] a failure and we need not repent to those

---

[6] Pannabecker, *Ventures of Faith*, 93.

[7] Ibid., 96.

whose money was spent, but to those who didn't receive enough to stay alive" in Elkhart-Goshen and around the world. Another letter, signed by many, expresses appreciation for music, but states that such organs are for concert performances, not for worship, and asks how "this instrument is consistent with our Anabaptist tradition of worship and style of life."[8]

Again President Waltner, in his calm and open manner, led in this crisis, of which the churches had been informed by the media. He explained how specially designated funds had been used to pay for it, and that he would take the issue to the seminary board. On March 12, 1970, the board expressed appreciation for this student concern and stated if the students were of one mind to have it shipped back to the factory, "we express our openness to listen to such a concern." But students remained divided, so the organ was installed. Many faculty and board members were proud of the students for their prophetic concern.

There were other issues, but these suffice to indicate the kinds of pressure the president worked under. An angry letter by students, which Erland Waltner and Ross Bender also signed, was sent to President Richard Nixon, with copies to the press, calling on him to end the Vietnam war, also led to negative ripples among the churches in late 1969. In response, Erland Waltner invited the Peace Section of MCC to lead the seminary in conversation on the war, which John A. Lapp did in a masterful way. As S. F. Pannabecker stated: "The year 1969–70 stands out as a kind of landmark.... It was the year graduates chose to celebrate commencement without the traditional caps and gowns and without the commencement procession; it was the first graduating class to have a member with a full bushy beard; it was the first class to have a woman graduate with the full three-year ministerial degree.... It was the end of the sixties and the beginning of the seventies."[9]

RELATIVELY QUIET WATERS

The coming of Ross T. Bender as dean to both seminaries in 1964 gave Erland Waltner some relief from administrative pressures. The GCBS move to Elkhart in 1969, when it became Goshen Biblical Seminary, brought further relief but also new challenges. Waltner spent the summer of 1966 on abbreviated sabbatical in Colombia, South America. As president of Mennonite World Conference (appointed in 1962) Waltner traveled extensively. In 1969 he visited a number of countries in Africa; in 1971 he traveled to Australia and the Far East. Then came

---

[8] Waltner collection, AMBS archives.

[9] Pannabecker, *Ventures of Faith,* 99.

MWC in Curitiba, Brazil, in 1972, where Million Belete of Ethiopia was chosen to succeed him. This gave Waltner more time for himself, for teaching and writing, as well as for speaking engagements. The president and dean worked exceptionally well together, which led to further expansion of curricular and seminary community options: the Overseas Mission Training Center; the Theological Center, responsible for bringing lecturers and Church-People-in-Residence to campus; new M.A. programs in Christian education, peace studies, theological studies, and later Christian formation.

A significant addition to the faculty team occurred when Marlin E. Miller came to the seminaries in 1974, after years in mission and MCC in Europe. He became visiting professor in theology during 1974–75, and was installed as president of GBS in 1975. This lightened the load for both Erland Waltner and Ross Bender. In 1990, Miller was installed as president of both seminaries, which together formed Associated Mennonite Biblical Seminaries (AMBS), a position he held until his untimely death in 1994. Soon after becoming president, Miller initiated the process of legal incorporation of AMBS, which was achieved in 1993.

Waltner retired from his leadership role at MBS in the summer of 1978 and was succeeded by Henry Poettcker as the president of MBS. The following year Waltner was in residence at Cambridge University in England. He returned to AMBS the fall of 1979 as professor of English Bible. One of his seminary catalog statements (1987–89) says: "My greatest joy continues to be proclamation and exposition of the Living Word (Jesus Christ) as known and understood in the Written Word (the Bible) and empowered by God's Spirit to illuminate and transform, and fulfill human life in all of its rich blossoming dimensions." Exposition and proclamation were part of the vision Waltner brought to his task at MBS in 1958.

Erland Waltner believed that in the calling, ordination, and installation of a minister, certain authority and power is given to the candidate: to preach with authority, and to have power to take initiatives and make decisions—though normally conferring with deacons, elders, and/or the congregation. During his long and effective ministry as pastor, teacher, and administrator, Waltner modeled and led Mennonites in setting the pastor free for the ministry to which God and Spirit have called him or her. A prophetic, dynamic, and fruitful ministry cannot happen without this freedom.

WAS THE VISION ACHIEVED?

After serving as president of MBS for twenty years, Erland Waltner continued teaching at AMBS until his full retirement. He must have felt a deep sense of satisfaction and gratitude to God for all that had been accomplished. GBS and MBS had become one school on one campus. They were receiving students and financial support from the churches in both conferences. Moreover, AMBS was often cited in later years as an example that the "Swiss" and the "Dutch" traditions could work together, an important factor in the eventual merging of the groups into one, Mennonite Church USA, on February 1, 2002. Unfortunately, no other Mennonite or related groups came to Elkhart, though their students there were many. For geographical and other reasons, two Mennonite seminaries were established later, one on the east coast and one on the west.

The initial faculty largely agreed with Waltner's vision, and a lively, disciplined academic community did emerge, teaching and publishing in the mode of both the academy and the church. With three graduates of Biblical Seminary in New York (which may have provided some of his model for MBS) joining Waltner on the faculty, the centrality of Scripture in the curriculum was assured, as was witnessing. As an excellent preacher and Bible teacher, the president had been much in demand throughout the AMBS constituency and beyond.

Meanwhile, a new faculty, with its own vision and agenda, succeeded the original one. The spiritual disciplines came with the 1980s or, more accurately, were recovered in the '80s from the Early Church and the Middle Ages, though glimpses appeared earlier at the seminary, often under the rubric of devotional literature. Waltner continues to serve as a spiritual director well into his eighties.

At Waltner's inauguration as president of MBS, the chairman of the board noted, "The task of an administrator is never easy. Problems loom up on every side." During his years in administration, Waltner had a wrench on every nut, i.e., he knew what was going on both on campus and in the churches, seemed to enjoy (or at least endure) endless committee meetings, and still managed to maintain a sense of humor. He worked hard. He seemed not to carry grudges. His classes were well attended; his personal relationships seemed to be excellent. He always made time for faculty who wanted to talk to him. He knew as much as a president needs to know about finances. He knew how to receive and solicit counsel, and how to delegate responsibility. He enjoyed the confidence of most of the faculty and the board, as well as of the churches. Indeed, in his office as president, he embodied many traits that constitute an outstanding leader.

In these years as president, Waltner was both obedient learner and obedient messenger—both disciple and apostle. His work at AMBS belonged to Jesus the Living Word.

3 | *From Kitchener to Curitiba*
Erland Waltner's presidency of Mennonite World Conference

Ross T. Bender

"JESUS CHRIST IS LORD. *JESUS CHRISTUS IST DER HERR."* With these words, Erland Waltner opened the seventh assembly of Mennonite World Conference. It was 2:00 p.m., Wednesday, August 1, 1962, in Kitchener, Ontario. Because of illness, the conference president, Harold S. Bender, had not yet arrived, and in his absence vice president Waltner presided and welcomed the participants.

The theme of the conference was "The Lordship of Christ." These words were written large and placed high above the stage so that all could see and none could forget. Above this banner was another that said "Seventh Mennonite World Conference." By the second day of the conference the position of the two signs had been reversed and "The Lordship of Christ" was elevated to the top spot. The symbolism could not be missed. Jesus Christ is Lord over the Mennonites of the world.

Another symbolic act occurred when, on the opening night, the lights were lowered, a spotlight shone on a portrait of the queen as the Canadian national anthem was broadcast. Many objected that this act betrayed an incipient spirit of nationalism that had no place in a gathering of a people who confessed that Jesus Christ is Lord. A second time we were reminded that Jesus Christ is Lord over the kingdoms and rulers of this world.

Registration for the conference totaled 12,207 people, and others dropped in for one or more sessions. Approximately 500 non–North Americans from at least twenty-five countries were in attendance.

Conference secretary C. J. Dyck attended to the many logistical details of the conference and was sensitive to the subtle and not-so-subtle symbolic actions that enhanced or detracted from the message of

Ross T. Bender is dean emeritus of Associated Mennonite Biblical Seminary, Elkhart, Indiana. He served as president of Mennonite World Conference from 1984 to 1990.

the theme. Presiding over the whole event in his calm, cool, and collected manner was Erland Waltner.

Waltner also presided over the daily sessions of the presidium whose role during the conference was to monitor the functioning of the day's sessions and to keep everything going according to plan. In addition to Bender and Waltner, the presidium included vice presidents H. W. Meihuizen (Netherlands) and Peter Wiens (Paraguay); treasurer Harold Schmidt (Canada); executive secretary C. J. Dyck; and members J. B. Toews (USA), Theo Glück (Germany), Paul Schowalter (Germany), G. H. Penner (Canada), Archie Penner (USA), I. I. Friesen (Canada), B. J. Braun (USA), E. J. Swalm (Canada), J. R. Barkman (USA), J. B. Martin (Canada), E. G. Steiner (USA), Hans Nussbaumer (France), Pierre Pelsey (France), and Samuel Gerber (Switzerland).

These weighty brethren, with many others listed on the program, were a veritable Who's Who of Mennonite men. As we look back four decades later, we are struck by the absence of African and Asian representatives on the presidium. Nor were there any women in that body. Further, it included no lay delegates or delegates of any other kind. The leaders of the world body of Mennonites were a small group of North American and European men appointed by their respective conferences. Under the leadership of Erland Waltner the composition of the governing structures would change radically in the following years.

The Kitchener meeting was not the first MWC gathering in which Erland Waltner participated. He gave a major address at the 1948 sessions (in Goshen, Indiana, and North Newton, Kansas) on the theme, "The Christian's Personal Religious Life." The third MWC assembly had been held in Amsterdam in 1936 on the 400th anniversary of Menno Simon's conversion. The fourth assembly was to be held in the United States but had to be canceled because of World War II. It was not until twelve years later, in 1948, that the fourth world conference was convened.

The fifth conference was held near Basel, Switzerland, in 1952. It was the first conference session that had official delegates, about 200 in number, of which 112 were North Americans with the rest being apportioned among the European conferences.

Erland Waltner also attended the sixth MWC conference in Karlsruhe, West Germany, and again gave a major address on the theme, *"Der Dienst der Mennoniten Gemeinden im Namen Christi an den Völkern"* (the service of the Mennonite churches in the name of Christ to the peoples of the world). The overall theme for the entire conference was "The Gospel of Jesus Christ in the World." In addition to the delegates from Europe and North America, this assembly made provision for five delegates from South America and three from Asia. It is not clear why there were no delegates from Africa.

Christian Neff of Germany had given leadership to MWC in its early years. When Neff died in 1946, Harold S. Bender succeeded him as the conference's guiding spirit. After Bender's death in 1962, the presidium turned to Erland Waltner. He was well prepared for the role of president, having served on the presidium since 1957, having participated in several assemblies, and having led the Kitchener sessions in 1962. He was well known and highly regarded as a church statesman among the Mennonites not only in North America but also around the world. During his years as president, he visited Mennonite churches in twenty countries on five continents.

The years leading up to his presidency had seen a gradual development of organizational structures, beginning with the charismatic leadership of Christian Neff. A preparatory commission planned and implemented the 1952 sessions in Switzerland. In 1957, a constitution was adopted that provided for a presidium or general council, a smaller executive committee, and a delegate body. As the years went by, the delegate body became more representative of the worldwide fellowship of Mennonites. Erland Waltner was president during the major changes in the makeup of the conference as the Mennonite World Conference became a worldwide body. Visually, the explosion of colors and costumes worn by delegates from six continents gave testimony to the dramatic changes among Mennonites of the world that have taken place in recent years.

Waltner's first major assignment as president was to give leadership to the planning for the eighth MWC assembly to be held in Amsterdam in July 1967. The theme chosen was "The Witness of the Holy Spirit." In the foreword to the proceedings of the eighth assembly, Waltner wrote, "While some were eager to explore the theological dimensions of the identification of the Holy Spirit in human experience, others were more concerned about the application of the Word of the Spirit to the burning human issues of our time. Both dimensions of the theme were amply provided for in the total conference program."

One issue that surfaced during the Amsterdam meetings was the bitterness left from World War II because of German mistreatment of the Dutch. The woman who hosted the Waltners acknowledged that she had not forgiven the Germans for killing her husband. She observed that her first reaction on seeing a German Mennonite leader listed as the preacher in the evening service was, "There's another of those damn Germans." However, she attended the service, was deeply moved by his sermon, and found healing for her bitterness.

Waltner opened the assembly with the presidential message, "The Fellowship of the Holy Spirit." In it he identified characteristics of that fellowship that were evident not only in the life of the New Testament church but which could also define the church today: vitality and power, unity and diversity, witness and service, freedom and order. Another highlight of the week was a sermon by Vincent Harding, "The Beggars Are Marching." The congregation responded with a standing ovation, their "Amen" to Harding's moving message, and a recognition that a prophet had spoken the word of the Lord in their midst.

After the close of the assembly, Erland Waltner and several other conference leaders traveled to East Germany to meet with a group of Mennonites who were unable to get permission to attend the meetings in Amsterdam. More than a hundred attended an all-day service in East Berlin. The communist authorities refused permission to the visitors to preach but did grant permission for them to pray. Those gathered were aware that the authorities had representatives present to monitor what was going on. We have no written record of what was said in these prayers, but it would not be surprising if the boundaries between praying and preaching were not observed too strictly.

Waltner was re-elected for another term as president following the Amsterdam assembly and gave leadership to the planning for the ninth MWC assembly in Curitiba, Brazil, in July 1972. This was the first full-fledged assembly not held in Europe or North America. There had been a meeting of Asian Mennonites in Dhamtari, India, in 1971, which Waltner had attended. It was the first meeting of what came to be known as the Asia Mennonite Conference and included representatives from Japan, Taiwan, Hong Kong, India, Indonesia, and Australia.

The theme chosen for the Curitiba assembly was "Jesus Christ Reconciles." As it turned out, the theme was timely, as reconciliation became a living reality and not simply a theoretical matter. Strong opinion, coming primarily from the Netherlands, objected to holding the assembly in Brazil in light of certain developments in Brazil's political life. C. J. Dyck and J. A. Oosterbaan met for a week in Curitiba with several Brazilian brethren to resolve the issues. While members of this group did not achieve complete unanimity, they were sensitive to the pleas of Brazilian Mennonite leaders that they not be abandoned by the world Mennonite fellowship in their hour of need. The presidium approved their recommendation to confirm the plan to meet in Brazil.

During the conference, several younger Latin American participants continued to express dissent and proposed to show their displeasure at the time of a communion service. Waltner, Dyck, and others used their diplomatic skills to keep the peace and work toward reconciling people with opposing points of view, at least for the time being. The conference proceeded to its conclusion without further dissent and without creating problems for the host churches in relation to their government.

Erland Waltner presented the keynote address at the opening service of the conference, "Jesus Christ Reconciles." In his masterful way, he not only developed this theme theologically but also illustrated the contemporary relevance of this motif that is at the heart of the gospel.

Another major issue that emerged at Curitiba concerned the future of MWC as an organization. Some people, primarily from North America, proposed that MWC had served its purpose and that the time had come to disband it. Some suggested that it be replaced by regional conferences. Those present vigorously debated this issue. Delegates from the two-thirds world contended that they were only now coming into closer fellowship with brothers and sisters around the world, that they needed closer ties with the rest of the Mennonite family, and that they had much to learn and much to teach as they were moving out of their period of dependence into equality with the western churches. In the end, the vote was strongly in favor not only of continuing MWC but of strengthening the organization, including its financial base. In the spirit of making the conference a more international (world) body, Erland Waltner declined to continue as president in favor of electing a president from the two-thirds world. That person was Million Belete from Ethiopia. Paul N. Kraybill was appointed executive secretary on a part-time basis (eventually full time), to carry out some of the wishes of the delegates for strengthening the organization.

The introduction to the proceedings expresses appreciation to all who made the Curitiba meeting a success. It draws attention to the leadership of Erland Waltner "whose sensitivity and statesmanship have been a beautiful gift of God to the world brotherhood." At the conclusion of the conference—the conclusion of his term of service—Waltner blessed those assembled with a benediction from Ephesians 3:20–21: "Now to him who by the power at work within us is able to do far more abundantly than all that we ask or think, to him be glory in the church and in Christ Jesus to all generations, for ever and ever. Amen."

4 | *Executive secretary of Mennonite Medical Association*

"**A**FTER SERVING WITH SEVEN MENNONITE MEDICAL
Association (MMA) presidents over a period of thirteen
years, Erland Waltner retired as executive secretary of
MMA at the 1992 convention at Laurelville. His administrative
experience as president of Mennonite Biblical Seminary, his knowledge
of church structures and leaders, and his belief in the mission of MMA
all combined to give MMA thirteen years of excellent leadership. In
gratitude, Erland was made an honorary life member of MMA."[1]

"Interest and timing," Erland Waltner answered when asked how it
happened that he accepted appointment as executive secretary of
Mennonite Medical Association in 1979. Erland's acceptance was a gift to
the life of MMA, as became ever clearer in the next thirteen years. Even
today, his pastoral ministry to Anabaptist physicians continues through
his regular column in the pages of *Mennonite Health Journal*.

Interest? Few people know that medicine was one of Erland's
possible career choices when he began college. Though he soon changed
directions, his interest in health and medicine were always present in his
thinking and writing, as one notes from many references to his holistic
understanding of shalom in many settings.[2]

Timing? Erland turned sixty-five and, having just retired from the
presidency of Mennonite Biblical Seminary, wisely decided to absent
himself from the campus for a year in deference to his successor. He and

---

Willard Krabill is a retired family practice physician from Goshen, Indiana. He served as
one of the Mennonite Medical Association presidents and succeeded Erland Waltner as
executive secretary.

[1] From the preface of *History of the Mennonite Medical Association: A Supplement. The 1991–
1997 Years* (Mennonite Medical Association, 1997), 20.

[2] See, for example, his article, "A Biblical/Theological Perspective on Pastoral Care," in this
volume on pages 68–75. See also his chapter, "Where Do We Go From Here?" in *Medical
Ethics, Human Choices: A Christian Perspective*, ed. John Rogers (Scottdale: Herald Pr., 1988),
143–51; reprinted in this volume on pages 76–82.

Winifred were enjoying a sabbatical year in England when the president of MMA, Art Kennel of Mayo Clinic, contacted Erland to invite him to serve half-time as executive secretary of this inter-Mennonite physicians organization founded in 1947.

With Erland's broad knowledge, insight, and experience in leading the seminary, the General Conference Mennonite Church, Mennonite World Conference, and other inter-Mennonite initiatives, he was able to lead MMA into even broader service and interaction with the broader Mennonite, Brethren in Christ, and Church of the Brethren constituencies.

Erland freely comments on how he benefited as well from the work with MMA. At the MMA convention in 1982 he took the health risk assessment, Project Renew, and discovered he was at risk and in need of some lifestyle changes. He and Winifred changed their eating, exercise, and stress management habits, and the benefits to them were prompt and lasting. Now, at 88, they eat healthily and continue almost daily walks. Erland described these life-changing decisions in an article in *Christian Living*, "To Be a Disciple May Mean to Jog."[3]

Each MMA president who served during Erland's tenure commented with admiration that Erland subscribed to the prestigious *New England Journal of Medicine*, and read from it regularly! He wanted to know what was going on in the world of medicine and wanted to be conversant with the issues being dealt with by members of the profession he served. It was a remarkable demonstration of Erland's thorough preparation for his tasks.

Among other rewards Erland identifies from his years with MMA is an appreciation for the stresses and biomedical ethical dilemmas faced by physicians. One outcome of this concern was his leadership in the 1982 joint study (with Mennonite Health Services and Mennonite Mutual Aid), "The Ethical and Stewardship Dimensions of Rising Health Care Costs." This study was only one of several MMA initiatives to address inequities in health-care access.

Erland also derived much inspiration from convention speakers, such as Paul Brand, William Bartholome, Everett Koop, and others. Preparing for the annual convention was stressful, but both Winifred and Erland found the meetings to be times of shared inspiration and renewal. There was one convention, however, that Erland found a little too stressful. He likes to tell the story of the last convention for which he was responsible, that of 1992, when he was concluding his MMA service.

---

[3] Erland Waltner, "To Be a Disciple May Mean to Jog," *Christian Living* (February 1984), 11–12.

After the evening service, on a hot June night, an exhausted 78-year-old Erland fainted, falling into the arms of the man who was to be his successor, Willard Krabill. Now that was a dramatic transition!

Early in his tenure with MMA, Erland became aware that he was being perceived as a pastor to Anabaptist physicians, especially to the succession of executive committee members. He grew into this role in a marvelous way, and through his articles in *Mennonite Health Journal* Erland continues in that ministry.

Although the impact of Erland's leadership was noted throughout the MMA membership, it was most personally felt by the officers who worked directly with him, including John Bertsche, Milton Claassen, Joe Duerksen, George Horst, Jep Hostetler, Willard Krabill, Joseph Longacher, Jr., and Herbert Myers.[4]

Some common themes and characteristics of Erland's leadership are gleaned from these officers. They note Erland's thoroughness and organizational gifts, his theological abilities, the way he became knowledgeable in the field of medicine, his application of principles of healthy living to his own life, and his humble nature while leading significantly. They express appreciation for the way Erland enhanced MMA's identity and mission as a church- and faith-based professional organization, helped MMA members view their practice of medicine through lenses of faith, was an encourager, and stretched himself by taking on leadership of a bunch of physicians in his retirement years. They characterize Erland as possessing a winning combination of personality, character, and giftedness—a ready smile, a twinkle in the eye, and a warm and winsome manner that invites and affirms others. In their experience, Erland was a teacher who brought fresh insights to Bible passages, and an administrator whose style combined an agile mind, careful attention to detail, thoughtful creativity, and shared responsibility. Also noted was Erland's clear leadership in matters of business and finance, but always in the context of the organization's larger vision. Erland combined a commitment to push MMA to expand its horizons with a keen insight and concern for the spiritual and emotional well-being of MMA members. He was always concerned about the ethical issues in medicine and their relatedness to the Anabaptist vision and mission. His meditations during planning sessions were insightful, inspiring, pertinent, and sensitive to each member of the group involved. Scholarly, articulate, graced with wisdom, Erland has a pastor's heart.

---

[4] My thanks to these former officers who contributed to this chapter.

All who worked with Erland spoke of the advantage he brought the organization: his wide acquaintanceship with the Anabaptist world, his comfort with a varied constituency, always working toward common goals, and a deeper understanding of the call to the ministry of healing. This familiarity was coupled with a wide knowledge of national and international issues that was most helpful in arriving at a balanced viewpoint in the statements MMA made to government and to society at large—policy statements well grounded in Scripture and in the life and teachings of Jesus. His was a steadying presence, capably representing MMA interests to the wider church and its agencies.

The two executive secretaries who succeeded Erland, Willard Krabill (1992–1996) and Jep Hostetler (1996–present) summarize Erland's work as follows: spiritual insights, global vision, cooperative attitude, and sincere hospitality are some of the earmarks of Erland Waltner's guidance of the Mennonite Medical Association from 1979–1992. Under Erland's leadership MMA branched out into international exchange and fostered spiritual growth, cooperative ventures, and renewal of the association.

China Educational Exchange

With the encouragement of J. Lawrence Burkholder, former president of Goshen College, Erland encouraged the formation of the China Educational Exchange in the 1980s. From 1982 to 1991 North American MMA members hosted thirteen Chinese physicians, and Chinese physicians from the Sichuan Medical College hosted twelve MMA members sent to them on teaching missions. Erland was instrumental in setting up the program, corresponding with candidates, and otherwise implementing the exchange.

Editorials and spiritual direction

Over the past twenty-three years, Erland has written forty editorials or spiritual insight pieces for *Mennonite Medical Messenger* and its successor, *Mennonite Health Journal.* The current editor of *MHJ*, Molly Hastings, said, "Erland Waltner is one of the most deeply spiritual persons I have ever met, and his writings communicate this depth." In the most recent issue of the journal, Erland writes, "The renewed mind is able to embrace not only brothers and sisters, but also the stranger and even the enemy. Contrary to prevailing cultural opinion, the love of enemies, and seeking peace with them, is the mark of a healthy, rather than unhealthy mind.... Let us be open to renewed minds, which can transform our lives Godward."[5]

This attitude of compassion, spiritual clarity, and Godward direction was a hallmark of Erland's leadership of MMA. He had the gift of offering words of spiritual wisdom and encouragement at pivotal points in the association's history.

Cooperative ventures

When Erland became executive secretary of MMA, following the 1979 convention, he became the first official representative of MMA to Mennonite Health Assembly. A new era of cooperation, collaboration, and informational exchange had begun. His active involvement in inter-Mennonite agency conversations paved the way for future interaction with Mennonite Health Services, Mennonite Mutual Aid, and other Anabaptist agencies. Erland was also instrumental in arranging an international gathering of Mennonite physicians at both the Strasbourg (1984) and Winnipeg (1990) Mennonite World Conferences.

MMA self study

Erland was aware of a waning interest in MMA on the part of some (especially younger) Anabaptist physicians, and under his direction a major self-study was conducted in 1980–81. The results of this study enabled the executive committee over the next number of years to find ways to energize the association. Erland and president Joseph Longacher, Jr., used this document in 1990 to draw up long-term objectives. The current operation of MMA is largely based on the insightful and cooperative work of these two men.

Student Elective Term

Although this program was started before Erland's tenure, he gave it added momentum. He cites this program as one of the highlights of his MMA term. It continues to arrange mission hospital sites and provide travel subsidies to medical students who volunteer to serve an overseas elective of six to eight weeks during their junior or senior year of medical school.

REGIONAL MEETINGS

Erland helped organize and went to great lengths to attend regional gatherings of MMA members in various communities. He enjoyed

---

[5] Erland Waltner, "Boundaries of Love," *Mennonite Health Journal* 3 (July-September 2001): 7.

meeting physicians who had not been able to attend any of MMA's annual national conventions.

Erland and Winifred Waltner were special guests at the 2001 Mennonite Medical Association/Mennonite Nurses Association convention at Laurelville Mennonite Church Center. At 87 years of age, Erland delivered a moving, one-of-a-kind, unforgettable message: "Theological Reflections on the Limits of Cure." Because of failing eyesight, he prepares his work on a magnifying monitor in his office. He delivered this outstanding message without notes because he could not have seen them.[6] This message illustrated his leadership style: Look at all the options, consider the basis on which decisions will be made, and move Godward in carrying out our mission.

One former MMA president spoke for all of us when he wrote; "I will always remember Erland as a gentle, firm, courageous, wise, and good man with whom I was privileged to be closely associated for a few short years. Thank you, Erland."

---

[6] See "Boundaries of Love" on pages 95–96 of this volume.

5 | *An office by the river*

NINA BARTELT LANCTOT

They that are planted in the house of the Lord
shall flourish in the courts of our God.
They shall bear fruit even in old age.
Vigorous and sturdy shall they be,
declaring how just is the Lord,
my rock, in whom there is no wrong. (Ps. 91:12–15)

ERLAND WALTNER HAS LIVED HIS LIFE IN THE CHURCH, in the house of the Lord, moving only from room to room as the Lord has led him. In the past decade of his life, as he has become more officially retired, God has furnished Erland with a new room in God's house. You will find him in the office of spiritual direction, a place of reflection, writing, and prayer. It is a room with a river view. In Erland's words,

> *During the last decade of my life…I am again in transition in my experience of God…. In this transition I am aware that for many years of my Christian life and ministry, my time with God was something like a quick stop while driving hard on a long and sometimes rough road. I have compared it to a pit stop in the Indianapolis 500…. Now I am beginning to see my relationship with God as being more like a river which helps me get from here to there, and also actually helps carry me along from day to day, from task to task, from one experience to the next.* [1]

God has led Erland from a spirituality of the road to a spirituality of the river. From an active life of congregational and denominational leadership, which often kept him literally on the road, God has planted him in the river—the stream of spiritual renewal embodied in the ebb and flow of spiritual disciplines, spiritual direction, and intercession.

The river of Christ-centered spirituality carries Erland on a small yet deep daily and weekly course. He has severely limited vision because

---

Nina Bartelt Lanctot is associate pastor of Belmont Mennonite Church, Elkhart, Indiana.

[1] "From Road to River Spirituality," in *Godward: Personal Stories of Grace*, ed. Ted Koontz (Scottdale: Herald Pr., 1996), 176. This piece is printed on pages 83–6 of the present volume.

of macular degeneration and lives his life in tune with God's motion close to his home across Benham Avenue from the campus of Associated Mennonite Biblical Seminary. He begins his daily rounds with a walk in the mall nearby.

God has established in Erland and Winifred's home, in addition to their ongoing ministry of hospitality, a rule of prayer to frame each day. When Erland returns from his morning walk, they read together and pray in response to the Moravian texts, a collection of Scripture reflecting Erland's youth and traditions. In the evening, they close the day with Scripture readings and prayers based on *Daily Light*, a resource Winifred became familiar with during her years in China. They are life partners in discerning whom to pray for (more Erland's approach), whom to write (more Winifred's approach), petitioning for the peace of the world.

Faithful routine characterizes Erland's weekdays. He keeps regular office hours at AMBS. He reads e-mail from correspondents around the globe, keeps abreast of the church's peace mission and denominational politics, is available for spiritual direction contacts or meetings, and provides a gentle, prayerful presence and many gifts of encouragement in the halls of the seminary.

Erland attributes much of his focus in the last decade to his continued learning at AMBS in the classes of Marcus Smucker. In the late 1980s, Marcus invited Erland to assist in the spiritual formation class, a basic orientation to the classic spiritual disciplines of prayer, contemplation, reflection, journal writing, and Sabbath keeping. Through his willingness to help by leading small accountability groups, Erland learned the value of rooting life in these disciplines. Then he began to teach the class "Spiritual Disciplines: Scripture." In the process, he learned the art of spiritual direction by teaching and observing, then by receiving. During this time, Erland began meeting with spiritual directors, first with Mary Herr, and later with Phyllis Carter, Diane Zaerr, and now with me.

One of the landmarks of Erland's recent years was the publication of his rich Believers Church Bible Commentary on 1 Peter. Erland acknowledges that the gift of spiritual direction with Mary Herr enabled this project to find completion between 1994 and 1999. In his desire to discern God's will among many "irons in the fire," he listened to Mary's counsel to say no to other commitments in order to focus on his scholarly passion. The commentary is a wonderful reflection of his love of God, Scripture, and the church.

Even as he focused on writing the commentary, another significant ministry was forming in Erland's life. The mysterious voice in the motion picture *Field of Dreams* beckoned a farmer to build a baseball field: "If you build it, they will come." As Erland obediently gave himself to practicing the presence of God, grounded in spiritual disciplines and spiritual direction, students and others began to seek him for their own direction. Some came by the referrals of Marcus Smucker and Marlene Kropf. Some just seemed to appear at his office. Erland has met with dozens of people over the last decade, listening along with them for God's guidance, for God's river, in their lives. Some have been seminary professors and students; others have been pastors, members of the local community, people from a variety of denominations and nations.

Christian believers hope that we will take on the character of the God of Jesus Christ as we walk in Christian faith. Erland has written, "I am experiencing God as One who is not only daily present with me but One who is in motion, bearing me up, sustaining, renewing, enabling me."[2] The very attributes of God that have sustained and guided Erland find expression in his ministry to those who receive his spiritual companionship and prayer.

One former AMBS student who now serves abroad describes Erland as "someone so rich in experience with church work and all the stresses that can accompany it, a man of God. Because of his personal walk with the Lord and pastoral heart he serves as a spiritual model for me. He has become our spiritual papa, as the people here would say."

Hazel Knicely Shirk, a pastor of the Bay Shore congregation in Sarasota, Florida, writes, "Erland seemed comfortable being around me, a woman of strength, who had traveled an unusual journey. My emotions were strong but he did not shrink from my pain or my accomplishments, my questions or my certitude. He was not afraid of me." As Hazel recalls a particularly painful part of her journey, she remembers Erland saying, "I am not a sadist. I don't get joy out of your pain." She goes on to say, "As I later took a walk it seemed that I was hearing from God. This God, whose Son suffered and died so that God's plan of redemption could be accomplished and who said that martyrs were blessed could also say, 'I'm not a sadist. I don't get joy out of your pain.' This experience helped me begin to feel that God is gracious and righteous and full of compassion (Ps. 116:5)."

Students looking for resonance with a more evangelical faith often found that in Erland. Deb Hewitt, an AMBS student with a Baptist background, writes, "Erland represented for me the openness and acceptance of God. He listened with an open heart to whatever I brought, ever encouraging me to bring everything to God."

[2] Ibid.

People with a passion for peace also found understanding in Erland. Ed Nyce, peace worker in Israel, wrote: "Erland's life compass seems almost naturally to be pointed toward God, though I am sure that such compass pointing is not automatic for Erland or for anyone else. His mind is consistently 'set on things above' (Col. 3:1–4). It is thrilling and hope-giving to see that Erland does all this in a way that is relevant for rather than dismissive of the everyday challenges and questions of life. His willingness to admit that not everything in life makes sense to him either, while simultaneously exuding joy and confidence in God, leads me to feel that I am being gently and firmly invited to share in the same journey."

Other directees found affinity in Erland's experiences in teaching and administration. Allen Dueck, principal of Bethany Christian Schools, writes, "One of the persistent themes in our monthly conversations has been, 'Where have you seen God in your life?' I find Erland's elder role particularly beneficial. He has lived richly and well and invested himself fully in various ministries. Out of this wealth of experience he is now willing to share with me while I'm very much in the middle of leading a church institution that seeks to nurture young people toward Christian discipleship." While Allen noted that Erland's devotional style and his own are not the same, Erland's listening presence and understated counsel have grounded Allen in faith's perspective while he carries the weight of administrative responsibilities. The river that carries Erland, God's river, carries Erland's directees as well.

Grounded in the rhythm of daily prayers at home and in small group and congregational worship and prayer at Hively Avenue Mennonite Church, Erland's ministry extends beyond the presence of prayerful listening to the power of persistent intercession. Deb Hewitt felt the power of Erland's prayer for her. "In the words of Walter Wink, Erland prays in 'spiritual defiance of what is, in the name of what God has promised.' Erland taught me that the task is not to get God to do something for me, but to see what God is doing, so I could respond to it and participate and take delight."

Hazel Knicely Shirk recalls God's care through Erland's calls and prayers. "I married and moved to Florida. Erland continued being my spiritual director by telephone as I made this transition. Without knowing of my particular circumstances, he called me at least twice when I needed support. I felt it was God's way of taking care of me."

Another former directee writes about Erland as a man of prayer: "I shared with him my sorrows, my stresses. I had been severely disappointed and shocked by actions of fellow brothers and sisters in Christ. I needed to regain confidence in the power of prayer and in the joy of sharing Christ's love with others. Erland listened with much compassion and empathy, and affirmed me in my gifts. I remember distinctly going to a session all wound up and tense, and after he prayed for me, my tension suddenly disappeared. Erland is a man of effective prayer. As James 6:16 says, 'The prayer of a righteous man is powerful and effective.'"

In addition to completing a commentary and offering spiritual direction and prayer, Erland still speaks occasionally at denominational or seminary events or at Mennonite Health Association. God seems to use these connections as opportunities for Erland to share words of hope and encouragement for the church he loves.

His ministry for peace in the world remains strong. Soon after September 11 Erland wrote a short editorial based on Romans 12:21, "Overcome evil with good," for *Mennonite Health Journal*. After she received the piece, editor Molly Hastings called Erland, in tears. Her daughter's husband was in the World Trade Center towers at the time of the bombing, and though he survived, the trauma of that day was having painful repercussions for her daughter and her grandson. This call began a relationship by phone and e-mail of consolation and intercession by Erland, extending the gospel of peace in his own quiet way to a family of souls who desperately needed to hear and understand it. Ed Nyce notes with appreciation Erland's ongoing interest and intercession for his work for peace between Israel and Palestine.

A man who has served the Mennonite church in so many capacities over the years, Erland brings a dynamic presence to congregational life. Mick Sommers, Erland's pastor at Hively Avenue Mennonite Church, describes Erland as a "fountain of affirmation and support. He has an enormous pool of understanding and compassion that comes from his own life and experiences, both of pain and of success." In congregational life Erland is a regular teacher of adult Sunday school. "Last year he began his service as the junior deacon," Mick says with a smile. "It is hard to describe a church statesman of eighty-eight as 'junior' anything." Mick sees Erland as embodying the best of the term "churchman." His grace, compassion, and diplomacy have enabled him to have just the right words at times of transition, including the memorial services of colleagues and peers John Howard Yoder, Gertrude Roten, Jake Enz, and Orlando Schmidt.

Writing about spiritual friendships in *The Mennonite* in 1988, Erland observes, "Through spiritual friends we may know God's love more deeply, ourselves more accurately, and be formed, step by step, into

Christ's image for us."[3] Erland has been befriended by God in Christ and has extended that friendship to many through his life at home, his rich work on 1 Peter, through spiritual direction and intercession, through a passion for peace and through congregational life.

As his current spiritual director, I have been blessed to witness the fruits of Erland's response to God's call throughout his lifetime. Diane Zaerr, his former director, writes, "Erland's faith, his hard questions directed to God, his persistent belief that God has a purpose for his life in his eighties just as in his earlier years all provided a blessing to me and a model for my own spiritual life." A man of peace, Erland has allowed the river of God to run its course, to hold him, and through him to carry others as well. His is not a torrential stream but one that flows full of the power of God's Spirit.

In his inaugural address when he became president of Mennonite Biblical Seminary in 1958, Erland proclaimed a vision of balance. He advocated a balance between scholarship and spirituality. "The scholar is not applauded above the one who prays, nor the one who prays above the scholar, but here it is the scholar who prays." Almost forty-five years later, Erland embodies this vision. His dimming eyes may not be able to see the far reaches of the world he once traveled. But when he looks at the river that carries him on, he sees the Source. "The work is thine, O Christ."

---

[3] Erland Waltner, "Spiritual Friendship: What's That?" *The Mennonite* (June 28, 1988), 269.

Erland and Winifred Waltner, May 1991

Several of the AMBS faculty members in the spring of 1978: Howard Charles, Gertrude Roten, Millard Lind, Erland Waltner, Henry Poettcker, and Clarence Bauman.

Erland Waltner breaks ground for the first buildings on the Elkhart campus, September 3, 1957. Behind him are Nelson Kauffman and J. N. Smucker, members of the Joint Coordinating Committee of AMBS.

Erland Waltner (second from left) checks on construction progress for the AMBS administration/classroom building, 1958.

The Administrative Committee of AMBS, 1958: Erland Waltner, S. F. Pannebecker, Harold S. Bender, Paul Mininger

The seminary community joined Erland and Winifred Waltner in singing his favorite hymn, "The work is thine, O Christ," in a celebration of Erland's ordination, August 1998.

In 44 years of ministry with AMBS, Erland touched the lives of many students in informal as well as classroom settings.

Erland Waltner, president of MBS from 1958–1978, speaks with Nelson Kraybill who became president of AMBS in 1997.

MBS President Erland Waltner and GBS President Marlin E. Miller await the message from Howard Charles at the opening chapel service for the 1975–1976 school year.

Erland Waltner:
His Work

While the disciple
is in essence
the obedient learner,
the apostle
is in essence
the obedient messenger.

Erland Waltner
Mennonite Biblical Seminary inaugural address
October 1958

While open to deal with
historical critical issues,
I have followed
a hermeneutic of trust
more frequently than
a hermeneutic of suspicion.

Erland Waltner
Believers Church Bible Commentary on 1 Peter
1999

To abound in hope
when so many round me
wallow in despair
strikes me as a divine calling
precisely for such an ominous time as this.

Erland Waltner
The Mountain Lake Observer
October 1942

6 | *There is no peace*

ERLAND WALTNER

T HERE IS NO PEACE, SAITH THE LORD, UNTO THE WICKED (Isa. 48:22). Peace is the desire of millions today. Ask the boy in uniform, ask his sweetheart or wife at home, ask his graying parents. All agree that they are earnestly waiting for strife and war to cease. Deep in their hearts there is a longing for peace.

But peace does not come simply by wishing for it. Peace is a treasure so precious that it costs a tremendous price. Let no one think that peace comes as a cheap bargain. No, it cannot even be purchased by "blood, sweat, and tears." Its cost is far greater than that.

It is important that we realize that those who do not walk in the way of peace shall have no peace. Isaiah speaks of such when he says, "The way of peace they know not.... They have made them crooked paths; whosoever goeth therein shall not know peace." He makes it clear that for him who refuses to walk God's ways, that is, for the wicked, there is no peace. The wicked man can never have inner peace nor can a wicked society enjoy outer peace. It is true that ungodly men may declare an armistice when they become exhausted in their strife but a cessation of hostilities is not yet true peace.

True peace, according to the Scripture, is a gift of God. Its price was the blood, not of soldiers, but of the Lamb of God. Its condition for the individual is a humble acceptance of this gift from him who said, "My peace I give unto you, not as the world giveth, give I unto you." Its condition for a society is nothing less than an acceptance of Christ as the King of Kings and Lord of Lords. True peace comes when the Prince of Peace reigns.

Erland Waltner was pastor of Bethel Mennonite Church, Mountain Lake, Minnesota, from 1941 to 1949. From 1942–1945, during World War II, Erland Waltner wrote a weekly meditation in *The Mountain Lake Observer*. This meditation appeared on the April 2, 1944.

7 | *Basic principles in improving church and conference relationships*

ERLAND WALTNER

H AVE YOU EVER OBSERVED HOW MUCH ATTENTION the New Testament devotes to the problem of human relationships? Did not Jesus have much to say on forgiveness, and reconciliation, and brotherly love, and spiritual fellowship, and harmonious cooperation in the cause of his kingdom? The book of Acts records how even the early church was rocked by dissension over the ministrations to poor widows (ch. 6) and later over the Judaistic heresy (ch. 15). But it also records how the early church found solutions to its problems and moved forward in its life of creative Christian fellowship. Moreover, have you observed how often Paul addresses himself to the problem of Christian unity? Large blocks of 1 and 2 Corinthians are devoted to the effort to restore proper relationships in a church torn by party spirit. His letter to the Philippians touches the same problem in its fervent plea, "Have this mind in you which was also in Christ Jesus" (Phil. 2:5). Ephesians and Colossians are devoted almost entirely to the theme that the church is a body under the headship of Jesus Christ. Finally, the letters of James and Peter and John and Jude all speak pointedly to the need for right relationships in the Christian brotherhood.

Our theme is then not peculiarly modern, but it is as old as the church. Our problems are not uniquely our own, but are as universal as God's people. Our solutions therefore must not be sought in our own wisdom but in that which comes from above which, according to James, is "first pure, then peaceable, open to reason, full of mercy and good fruits, without uncertainty or insincerity" (3:17).

The topic assigned for this presentation is immense in its scope. Three levels of relationships properly enter the picture: (1) relationships within local churches, such as that between the minister and the congregation or the relationship among individual members or groups

Erland Waltner gave this message at the Western District Ministers' Conference, Zion Mennonite Church, Elbing, Kansas, in the spring of 1957. His text was Colossians 1:9–20.

within the congregation, (2) relationships of the local church to the conference, including both the district and the general conference levels, and (3) relationships among the churches within the conference, either as individual congregations or between groups of congregations.

Clearly, such a field for discussion is vast and complex. Moreover, here is an area in which we have "all sinned and come short of the glory of God." While we may manifest the spirit of Christ in many things, no church, no minister, and no individual member would claim that he has always been consistently Christ-like in all the areas of human relationships involved in our church and conference life. That is why we must devote ourselves to the improvement of these relationships. Here we shall attempt to suggest basic principles drawn directly from the Word of God which may guide us to better relationships.

THE PRINCIPLE OF CENTRALITY

John Ruskin in his essay on composition declared that all great art must observe what he called "the law of principality."

> The great object of composition being always to secure unity; that is, to make out of many things one whole; the first mode in which this can be effected is by determining that one feature shall be more important than the rest, and that the others shall group with it in subordinate positions.[1]

This principle applies not only in art in the usual sense, but also in the fine art of true church and conference fellowship. The church must have one head. Nature itself teaches us that a body must have but one head. A two-headed creature is always a monstrosity. Paul teaches the principle of centrality in both Ephesians and Colossians, especially in Colossians 1:18 where he says of Christ, "And He is the head of the church, who is the beginning, the first-born from the dead, that in all things He might have the pre-eminence."

No Christian would quarrel with Paul over this assertion. We all confess the pre-eminence of Christ. But, on the other hand, there is not a single church in our conference, nor a single individual in these churches, who does not encounter difficulty in living out this great affirmation. Our failure to live it out impairs our church and conference relationships. Let us consider some of the implications of this text.

If Christ is pre-eminent, the individual self should not be pre-eminent. In our Christian faith and especially in our Mennonite heritage we have made much of individualism. We have stressed the importance of the individual and the right of the individual to follow his own conscience and to interpret the Bible as he understands it. This emphasis

---

[1] Quoted in H. T. Kuist, *These Words upon Thy Heart* (Richmond: John Knox Pr., 1947), 163.

has its value, but an overemphasis upon the individual is both disruptive to our fellowship and contrary to the New Testament. The biblical spirit says, "Not I, but Christ." Christ is pre-eminent.

If Christ is pre-eminent, then the individual minister is not pre-eminent. The church of Corinth was divided because groups within the congregation had exalted human leaders too much, some being devoted to Paul, others to Apollos, and others to Cephas. Paul in writing to them explained that he had only planted, and Apollos had watered, but God had given the increase. An undue exaltation of individual ministers is not only divisive, but it dishonors the pre-eminence of Christ.

If Christ is pre-eminent, the local church is not pre-eminent. Local church autonomy is a cherished emphasis in our church polity. We hold that no pope, no ecclesiastical hierarchy, not even a conference board or a district committee has a right to dictate to the local church. But this does not mean that the local church may then go its own way without consideration for the convictions of other congregations, for the local church along with these other congregations is subject to the lordship of Jesus Christ.

But if Christ is pre-eminent, then the conference is not pre-eminent either, nor its institutions. We need to work toward the strengthening of conference loyalty, yet this must never be done at the expense of loyalty to Christ. We should be concerned about the loyalty of ministers and of churches to the conference, for ethically no one has a right to the benefits of the conference without giving loyal support to it. But in the same moment we should be even more concerned about the loyalty of our conference and its institutions to the Lord Jesus Christ. These two concerns of loyalty to conference and loyalty to Christ can never be separated as we seek to live out the pre-eminence of our Lord.

If Christ is pre-eminent, then our Mennonite heritage is not pre-eminent. When I say this I speak as one who is deeply appreciative of our history and heritage, as one who feels that we must do more and not less to understand and transmit this heritage, and as one who feels that it is folly to draw a contrast between Mennonitism and Christianity, simply because Mennonitism is Christianity as we have come to understand it. Yet we also realize that is possible for a group to begin to worship its past and to be bound by it, substituting its heritage for Jesus Christ and his eternal Word. Let us study our heritage. Let us appreciate it. Let us seek to transmit it, but always giving Christ the pre-eminence.

Church and conference relationships will be improved if all of us will not only profess but also live out the pre-eminence of Christ. An overemphasis on the individual, on the minister, on the local church, or even on the conference and our Mennonite heritage tends to divide us.

An emphasis on Jesus Christ tends to unite. In him, as Paul says, "all things hold together" (Col. 1:17).

THE PRINCIPLE OF BALANCE

When Paul was bidding farewell to the elders of Ephesus in Acts 20, he said that in his ministry there he had "kept back nothing that was profitable" (v. 20) and again that he had declared "the whole counsel of God" (v. 27). Paul proclaimed a full-orbed, well-rounded, and well-balanced Christian message which included all the essential elements. This remarkable characteristic of the message of Paul is also seen in his epistles in which the tenets of doctrine and the principles of ethics are presented in striking balance.

A wheel that moves not only needs a center but also spokes and a rim. Moreover, these spokes need to be the same length; otherwise the wheel will be unbalanced. Is this not another clue to the improvement of church and conference relationships? We know what happens when one spoke of a wheel is too short, or, for that matter, too long. We know how rough it would be to ride on a wheel like that. Perhaps that is what we have been trying to do.

Christ is indeed the hub of our church and conference wheel. But the various Christian doctrines issuing in their respective ethical expressions make up the spokes and the rim. If then we overemphasize one aspect of Christian truth at the expense of another, the wheel is unbalanced and goes "thump, thump, thump." If in the matter of doctrine we lengthen the spoke of nonresistant love at the expense of the new birth, or vice versa, we tend to unbalance the wheel. On the other hand, it may be that the wheel has been unbalanced in the past and that some spoke now needs lengthening in order to get the wheel to run more smoothly.

When any aspect of the Christian gospel is neglected, a spiritual vacuum is created which leads to disruptions in the fellowship. Neglect of the Holy Spirit feeds pentecostalism, neglect of the Bible feeds militant fundamentalism, neglect of the healing ministry feeds the healing cults. On the other side, when any aspect of the Christian truth is overemphasized and is separated from its gospel context, it becomes a heresy, at least in embryo.

In historical theology we recognize that an overemphasis on the humanity of Christ becomes a heresy, but so does an overemphasis on his deity at the expense of his humanity. Likewise, an overemphasis on human responsibility for salvation is a heresy as well as its counterpart which is an overemphasis on grace at the expense of human responsibility. Even nonresistance could become a heresy if it is overemphasized and separated from the gospel of salvation.

To achieve balance is no mere mechanical process, such as deciding to preach five sermons on the new birth and the same number on Christian love. The achievement of balance is a dynamic process which involves an intimate walk with the Lord and a diligent study of the Scriptures in their entirety. The key to proper balance is to be found in an approach to the Bible as a whole, where all the essential aspects of Christian truth are presented. But the achievement of balance also calls for an appreciation of all aspects of Christian doctrine and of all methods which the Holy Spirit uses to build up his church. It allows no place for prejudice against either evangelism or Christian education, or against the doctrine of the new birth or the doctrine of nonresistant love.

THE PRINCIPLE OF DISCRIMINATION

The early church was subject to many diverting pressures from within and from without. Heresy, either of the Judaistic or of the Gnostic variety, threatened the life and unity of the church repeatedly. Much of the New Testament was written to define true Christian doctrine and to develop in Christians a sense of discrimination. The counsel of Paul in 1 Thessalonians 5:21 was apt for his time and for ours: "Prove all things, hold fast that which is good."

To understand some of our church and conference problems we need to understand how our Mennonite people have been affected by a variety of outside influences which have descended on them through the radio, through visiting speakers, and through all kinds of books, pamphlets, and periodicals. At a Mennonite Cultural Conference at Hesston, Kansas, recently, Dean H. S. Bender spoke very helpfully on how Mennonites have been influenced theologically both from the side of theological liberalism and from the side of militant fundamentalism.[2] He made it very clear that damage had come to our fellowship not only from one but from both sources.

To see danger from one side alone and to be blind to danger from the other is to act on the basis of prejudice and not on the basis of discrimination. Discrimination means that we are able to look at any teaching or movement and on the basis of standards which we know to be valid determine what is true and what is false in them.

---

[2] Harold S. Bender, "Outside Influences on Mennonite Thought," in *Proceedings of the Ninth Conference on Mennonite Educational and Cultural Problems, held at Hesston College, Hesston, Kansas, June 18–19, 1953* (North Newton, Kans.: Council of Mennonite and Affiliated Colleges, 1953), 33–41.

Currently, the various varieties of ecumenicalism in our country are making a considerable impact on the thinking of many of our people. Some of our people are clearly following the line of the American Council of Churches, a militant fundamentalist group headed by Carl McIntire. Others are more inclined to seek fellowship in the National Association of Evangelicals, a more moderate fundamentalist group. Still others follow with eager interest all that happens in the National Council of Churches and rather deplore the fact that American Mennonites could not be officially represented at the 1954 World Council sessions in Evanston. Actually many of the tensions within our local church and in our conference, on such matters as the Revised Standard Version, for example, are primarily the projections of the conflicts which are going on among these larger ecumenical movements. Some of our people just tend to believe everything Carl McIntire says, and others tend to believe everything *The Christian Century* says, and too few have an adequate sense of discrimination to separate the chaff from the wheat in either case.

The development of discrimination, however, does not come through "ten easy lessons." This too means an intimacy with the Lord Jesus Christ, a thorough acquaintance with the Word of God, and an open-hearted reliance on the Holy Spirit which will enable us to detect both false doctrine and an unchristian spirit before too much damage is done. We must learn to look at all interpretations and movements through the eyes of the mind of Christ.

When we see a minister reading Reinhold Niebuhr or observe that he has the *Interpreter's Bible* on his shelf, we need not be so much worried if we know that he keeps his open Bible near at hand. Neither should we be disturbed if he reads Louis Sperry Chafer or Carl McIntire. But if he begins to substitute the writings of men—any men, whether modernists or fundamentalists, or neo-orthodox—for the Word of God, then we foresee only chaos and conflict ahead in our attempt to give a unified message and to maintain an integrated fellowship in our churches. We need to read widely, on all sides of controversial questions, but we also need to read with spiritual discrimination which will keep us from being cut loose from our moorings in Christ and his Word.

THE PRINCIPLE OF MATURATION

In a study of the life of the early church it becomes clear that one of the secrets of its cohesive and creative fellowship was the fact that it kept on moving forward. In Ephesians 4 Paul pleads for growth in the church, both upward and outward, "till we all come in the unity of the faith and of the knowledge of the Son of God, unto a perfect man unto the measure of the stature of the fullness of Christ, that we henceforth be no more children, tossed to and fro, and carried about with every wind of doctrine, by the sleight of men, and cunning craftiness, whereby they lie in wait to deceive; but speaking the truth in love, may grow up into him in all things, which is the head, even Christ" (4:13–15).

In one respect the community of believers is like a man riding a bicycle. He needs to remain in motion to stay upright. When he stops moving, he starts toppling. Right relationships in our churches and in our conference depend in part on whether we are moving ahead in our faith and in our service for Christ.

Does this not mean that we must be more diligent, as individuals and as churches, in studying the meaning of our faith and in applying it in our personal and group living? If we stop studying, we will start bickering. If we slacken our pace in serving, we are more likely to devote our energy to quarreling.

As Paul challenged the Ephesians to move forward in faith and life, so we too must forge ahead in our century that we may grow up into Christ in all things. Several years ago during the Eden Peace Study Conference the Spirit moved among us and already we have seen the fruit of the Spirit in greater unity among us. But we need intense study in many other areas—in evangelism, in church discipline, in our view of the Scriptures, in our interpretation of the Christian hope, and many others.

If we come to study conferences on these and similar subjects with an earnest desire to "grow up into Christ," such further gatherings could mean much to improve church and conference relationships.

THE PRINCIPLE OF COMMUNION

Emil Brunner has observed that a basic heresy of historic ecclesiasticism and perhaps also of modern ecumenicalism is that it has substituted the secular idea of "unity" for the biblical teaching of "communion." In his stimulating book, *The Misunderstanding of the Church*,[3] he argues that the church according to the New Testament is essentially not an institution, but a "fellowship of believers," a communion in and with Christ, a common participation in him who is our Savior and Lord. This is essentially what Anabaptists and Mennonites have always said. From his observation he draws the conclusion that our unity, therefore, is not to be sought simply on an institutional or organizational level, for this would be artificial and superficial. Our true unity is in our communion in Christ.

---

[3] Emil Brunner, *The Misunderstanding of the Church* (Philadelphia: Westminster Pr., 1953).

If Brunner is right, then another clue to the improvement of church and conference relationships lies in the cultivation of this communion in Christ.

Communion in this sense is the exercise of true Christian love and the practice of true Christian brotherhood. In this communion in Christ we do not seek to create unity, we simply recognize our oneness in Jesus Christ and permit his presence in our midst to control all our thoughts and words and deeds pertaining to each other. In this communion 1 Corinthians 13 becomes flesh and blood.

This means that each member of the church considers not only the general physical and spiritual welfare of others but also respects the conscience of other brethren. Such communion says with Paul, "If food is a cause of my brother's falling, I will never eat meat, lest I cause my brother to fail" (1 Cor. 8:13).

Communion in this sense is also sharing. It is a readiness to share freely with each other our experiences with Christ, and to discuss our agreements and our differences in a spirit in which we always "speak the truth in love." In this communion we are honest enough to speak the truth plainly, but we are also loving enough to speak it tenderly so that we are all edified and the bonds of fellowship are strengthened.

We observe the Holy Communion by partaking of the sacred emblems of the atoning work of Christ on the cross of Calvary. But at our conference sessions and on many other occasions we have opportunity to demonstrate the reality of our communion and to cultivate it by sharing with each other in the precious things of Christ and by working together lovingly in the planning of our conference program of service. This, rather than the Holy Communion, may be the real index of the health of our church and conference relationships.

In summary, here are five paths we need to take:

1. We need to live out more diligently the implications of the pre-eminence of Christ above our individualism, our ministerial authority, our local church autonomy, our conference loyalty, and our Mennonite heritage.
2. We need to regain and maintain a better balance in our doctrinal emphases and in our church and conference programs.
3. We need to develop discrimination in our response to influences which come to us from the outside.
4. We need to move forward in the study of our faith and of its implications for living and service in this twentieth century.
5. We need to deepen our communion in Christ by sharing together more freely our experience of Christ and by giving expression to our faith in our common fellowship and program of service.

Halford Luccock remarks that this generation may be characterized by the word "split."[4] We speak of the split atom, the split second, the split personality, split churches, and a badly split world. We as the church must be able to tell the world of Jesus Christ in whom all things hold together.

Martin Niemöller, giving his last lecture in a series at our seminary in Chicago, declared that the church has nothing really to fear from its "flesh and blood" enemies on the outside. We have the word of Christ for it that the gates of hell can never destroy the church. But, he added very soberly, there is something which can destroy the church and there is no guarantee even in the Scriptures against that. The church can be destroyed by us Christians from within if we fail to give Christ his rightful place of victorious pre-eminence. But this we must not do. This we will not do.

---

[4] Halford Luccock, *Communicating the Gospel* (New York: Harper, 1954), 92.

8 | *Education for apostleship*

ERLAND WALTNER

I F I MAY PREFACE MY PRESENTATION WITH A PERSONAL
word, it would be to bear testimony to the amazing grace of God in
my own life. It is God's holy love which has humbled and
encouraged me again and again, and it is God's sustaining presence
which I need most in this experience. Further I would recognize my deep
indebtedness to all who have gone before me in the love of the church
and in the life of the seminary. Here too, as Jesus said, the saying holds
true, "One sows and another reaps.... Others have labored and you have
entered into their labors." We are but links in a chain which is being
forged in a Hand that is not our own, involved in tasks so overwhelming
that none of us would choose them for ourselves.

The nature and strategy of theological education has been the
subject of much discussion in the last few years. This fact may indicate at
once both the crucial significance of our subject and also the current
confusion concerning it.

If Jesus Christ is the hope of humanity and the church is custodian
and dispenser of this message, then the significance of the training of
Christian ministers is second to that of no other task. Viewed from
within the framework of Christian faith there can be no greater nor more
demanding enterprise than the training of men and women to be faithful
servants of Jesus Christ.

But if these discussions indicate importance, they also reveal
confusion. There is, in fact, much confusion today concerning the true
nature of ministry and consequently also concerning the strategies by
which the training for ministry is to be achieved.

THE MEANING OF EDUCATION FOR APOSTLESHIP

This topic assumes at once that we are concerned with a process and a
purpose, with means and with ends. Theological education is *education*
and not something else. The seminary, as Walter N. Roberts told us at
our dedication service, is a school. The point of a school is learning

---

"Education for Apostleship" was Erland Waltner's address on the occasion of his
inauguration as president of Mennonite Biblical Seminary, October 26, 1958.

which takes place under the stimulation of teaching. In this respect the seminary is like, rather than unlike, any other educational institution.

Theological education derives a distinctive character primarily from the nature and content of its goals. Its objectives are distinctive. It moves forward, if it moves at all, as it pursues its own specific goals.

It is no accident that in the extensive study of theological education by the American Association of Theological Schools, the first reports addressed themselves to the questions of ends. This is done in the volume by H. Richard Niebuhr, Daniel Day Williams, and James M. Gustafson, entitled *The Purpose of the Church and Its Ministry.*[1] It is only after effective wrestling with the issue of aims that there can be meaningful handling of the problem of methods in theological education. This is done in the further volume entitled *The Advancement of Theological Education.*[2]

Our purpose here is not to add to or detract from what has been said helpfully in these volumes, but to address ourselves to certain aspects of theological education which are urgent and relevant in the particular enterprise of Mennonite Biblical Seminary. Even to attempt this at the beginning of one's administrative responsibilities must seem presumptive, yet what we say is shared as vision and aspiration which requires the seasoning of experience.

Addressing ourselves first to the issue of purpose, we speak here of Christian ministry in terms of apostleship. There are, of course, other categories under which we would properly and fruitfully describe Christian ministry.

When we speak of *apostleship* we do not intend to suggest a contrast to the more prevalent term *discipleship.* If the essence of Christian discipleship is obedient dedication of the whole life to Jesus Christ our Savior and Lord, then apostleship is but the acceptance of further responsibility which Christ places on the shoulders of those he calls into a special ministry of proclamation and service. While the disciple is in essence the obedient learner, the apostle is in essence the obedient messenger. The term apostle denotes "the sent one." As J. Y. Campbell puts it, "An apostle is one sent forth, a messenger, especially one authorized to act in a particular matter for the one who sends him."[3]

---

[1] H. Richard Niebuhr, *The Purpose of the Church and Its Ministry; Reflections on the Aims of Theological Education* (New York: Harper, 1956).

[2] H. Richard Niebuhr, *The Advancement of Theological Education* (New York: Harper, 1957).

[3] "Apostle," in *A Theological Word Book of the Bible,* ed. Alan Richardson (New York: Macmillan, 1950), 20.

To conceive of Christian ministry in terms of apostleship is to recognize the impelling significance of the Great Commission, the urgency of church evangelism, and the imperative of Christian witness in society. It is to see discipleship focused in terms of a responsible relationship to the world. It is to realize that Christ's "Go ye into all the world" is as crucial as his "Come ye after me." It is to acknowledge that while Christians in the world are not of the world, they are nevertheless sent forth into the world even as Christ was sent into the world. It is to see the church as an instrument of global mission, the voice of a great proclamation. It is to view the minister as a messenger seeking to bring both the tender invitation and the full counsel of God.

To lift up the apostolic character of the Christian ministry is not, however, to minimize other recognized aspects of this holy calling. As the church is called to minister to "the whole man," so a teaching ministry, a pastoral ministry, a liturgical ministry are all parts of this larger service. We may not all agree that it is best to call the modern minister a "pastoral director" as the Niebuhr report does, but we must surely agree that the pastoral and administrative functions of this ministry are necessary and vital. The dimension which this designation "pastoral director" seems to lack is the essential missionary quality of ministerial responsibility, the role of the ambassador who beseeches, in Christ's stead, "Be ye reconciled to God." To underscore this aspect of the minister's calling we thus speak of it as apostleship.

THE CONTEXT OF EDUCATION FOR APOSTLESHIP

If we should agree that the training of Christian workers may properly be called education for apostleship, we need now consider certain aspects of the educational process involved in the preparation of such ministers.

Here we shall not deal with the basic theological or psychological aspects of such preparation. We assume training for kingdom service is ultimately the work of God through the Holy Spirit. We also hold that in this process psychological aspects in the development of Christian personality are of crucial significance. We shall not deal here with such external matters as organization, administration, curriculum, faculty, physical facilities, and other related elements in theological education, important as these are.

We shall rather explore the kind of context in which such education for apostleship may take place effectively and fruitfully. By context we here mean primarily the atmosphere which is made up of values and attitudes, relationships and feelings, more than formal activities. This context involves certain polarities which we need to recognize and which may help give some sense of direction in our venture. The nature of these polarities is such that if we let go of either pole, we suffer loss. On the other hand, to cling to both is most difficult even while imperative. This makes seminary education both complex and challenging.

Freedom and commitment

Seminary training takes place, first, in the polarity of freedom and commitment. It involves both learning and believing, both inquiry and affirmation.

Education which is true to a Christian understanding of humanity can operate only in a setting which assumes and assures basic freedom. There must be freedom of inquiry, the possibility of an honest search for truth, the right to share convictions even when these may deviate from accepted norms. There must be respect for individual differences and concern for maintaining fellowship as well as for achieving consensus of thought.

On the other hand, the seminary as an arm of the confessing church of Jesus Christ is also characterized by commitment. A seminary cannot be satisfied with a concept of education which holds as its final ideal a situation in which "all questions are open, all assumptions tentative, all conclusions provisional."[4] In Christian perspective freedom is a high value but its realization occurs morally and intellectually in the context of a great commitment. "If ye abide in my word," said Jesus, "then are ye my disciples indeed, and ye shall know the truth and the truth shall make you free. If the Son shall make you free, ye shall be free indeed." The Christian seminary agrees with Gilbert Chesterton that the most important thing about knowing truth is to know the important truth. In Christian faith this means the acknowledgement of him who said, "I am the Way, the Truth, and the Life. No man cometh to the Father but by me."

In seminary we search for truth with the framework of this all-controlling and life-transforming commitment. Freedom in this context is freedom in Jesus Christ. The search for truth continues. The expedition is not ended with the confession that Jesus Christ is truth. The Christian student believes that "the Lord hath yet more light and more truth to break forth from His Word." In this perspective the seminary is not only a vehicle for the transmission of a glorious tradition or heritage, but it is also a laboratory and a workshop where God makes himself known in the present moment. The believer thus is still a learner and the learner is a believer. He studies, but as Walter Moberly puts it, "he studies on his knees."

---

[4] Wherever possible, we have identified the source of quoted material in this address. Where no attribution is given, we were unable to identify the source. *Ed.*

Education thus conceived is intricate and arduous. As Howard Lowry puts it in *The Mind's Adventure*, "Fact-collecting, open-mindedness as an end of life, to be forever learning and never coming to a knowledge of truth is less arduous than reflective commitment. Reflection is easy and commitment is easy, but the two together—that is an educational task requiring the highest powers."[5] It is in this task that we are engaged.

Scholarship and spiritual life

A second polarity includes concern for intellectual stimulation on the one hand and for spiritual nurture on the other. For a seminary to make a choice between scholarship and spirituality is fatal. To be committed to both is "the hard and narrow way" but it leads to life.

Sound, painstaking scholarship should be characteristic of the professors, the students, and the graduates of a seminary. If Luke in preparing to write his Gospel was scholar enough to "follow all things closely (or accurately) for some time past, in order that he might write an orderly account for Theophilus," then the Christian messenger in our day cannot afford to be satisfied with slovenly workmanship. Paul admonished young Timothy, "Do your best to present yourself to God as one approved, a workman who has no need to be ashamed, rightly handling the word of truth" (2 Tim. 2:15).

On the other hand, no seminary can afford to neglect the spiritual life, including the life of prayer. Dr. Samuel Shoemaker properly asks questions of seminaries and seminarians, "Where goes the glow?" Why is it that so often students who come to seminary with enthusiasm and zeal then lose their spiritual ardor before they are ready to graduate?

Wilbert Webster White once described the ideal of the Biblical Seminary in New York as "a movement that will produce a type of Christian leader who will be markedly superior in sacrificial service and who will conspicuously combine the characteristics of saint and scholar." To produce scholarly saints or saintly scholars is an objective worthy of any Christian training school, but neither the emphasis on scholarship alone nor the emphasis on spiritual nurture alone is adequate in training for apostleship.

Biblical studies and modern man

A third polarity in education for apostleship involves the relative emphasis placed on biblical studies and that placed on the "sciences of

---

[5] Howard Foster Lowry, *The Mind's Adventure: Religion and Higher Education* (Philadelphia: Westminster Pr., 1950).

man." The first pole centers in the content of the Christian message while the second pole is concerned about those to whom this message applies.

In the deliberate choice to name our institution a "biblical" seminary, we have already registered a commitment to the primacy of biblical studies in the making of a minister. We take this stand because we believe that the Bible is the inspired Word of God, the Christian's infallible guide for faith and life. We believe deeply with Peter T. Forsythe that "the Christian leader must know the Bible better than any other book." We hold with Wilbert Webster White that the curriculum of a Christian training school should be "biblio-centric," one that places the Bible at the center and keeps it at the center though the area around that center will involve every other field of study which is relevant to a better understanding of the Bible and a more effective use of it in Christian service. We would concur with Abdel Ross Wentz when he declared that our times call for "personalities drenched in the message of the prophets and apostles," that is, ministers thoroughly saturated with the Word of God.

But to declare this emphatically is by no means to minimize the significance of those studies which deal with an understanding of man and society. It is possible to so immerse oneself in certain types of biblical studies that one loses touch with the inner and the outer world of twentieth-century persons and thus faces the peril and prospect of being irrelevant. To know the nature of human beings and their needs, their behavior and the reasons for it, their thought forms and modes of expression, their predicaments and tragedies, their aspirations and hopes, to learn to see them in the tragedies and triumphs of their existence and beyond that to be able to enter into the inner human life with understanding and identification—all of this is also essential in the making of an effective minister. As Roger Hazleton has aptly put it, "Sometimes the king makes men into ministers; today it may well be thought of as making would-be ministers into men.... The true calling of the minister is to be a servant—and servanthood means self-identification with the needs and longings of others in one's own time and place."

Content and communication

A fourth polarity, closely related to the preceding, involves the balance between the theoretical studies and those which deal with the skills of communication. Shall the seminary seek to produce theologians or shall it seek to produce pastors and preachers and personal workers?

There are those who will champion the importance of mastering the biblical languages, of accumulating vast stores of historical information, of gathering theological ammunition so that one can carry on stimulating theological conversation on every thinker from Augustine to Bultmann. On the other hand, there are those who raise the disturbing question, What shall it profit a man if he shall gain a whole world of information about the Bible and human thought, if he can explain the meaning of Hebrew roots, recognize at sight any form of the Greek verb, be able to expound the meaning of existentialism and to discuss Kierkegaard and Heidegger, what shall it profit if he can do all these but does not have the love and the skill to bring one person to faith in Jesus Christ?

But to choose between the theologian and the evangelist would be as wrong as trying to classify the Apostle Paul in the one category or the other. Paul was obviously both. C. S. Lewis is right when he insists that all are already theologians if they do any thinking about God at all. The real difference is that some are very bad theologians while others think of God more clearly and more correctly. For the Christian minister in the modern world, basic theological disciplines can scarcely be considered optional. Of early Christians it was said that they out-thought as well as out-lived and out-died pagans. It is unlikely that Christianity today can remain a vital force and become once again a conquering power apart from the strenuous discipline which careful theology requires.

But theoretical study in a seminary is never to be divorced from practical ends. Unless the theologian is concerned about communicating Jesus Christ and is able in some way to do so, he may well fall under the condemnation of Kierkegaard who insisted that it was the theologians of his day who were crucifying the Son of God afresh. William A. Clebsch, in the current issue of the *Canadian Journal of Theology*,[6] is right in pleading fervently and effectively that the mission of the church must be the context of all theological education. "The entire range of theological study, from Hebrew to Homiletics," he says, "must take as its ruling context the mission of the people of God in the world."

Denominationalism and ecumenism

Finally, education for apostleship in our situation needs to take place in the polarity of loyal church-relatedness on the one hand and open Christian conversation on the other. Is it possible for Mennonite Biblical Seminary, or any denominational seminary, to be true to its own commissioning by its constituency and also be properly involved in the issues of the larger Christian fellowship in the world? We believe that this is not only possible but imperative.

---

[6] William A. Clebsch, "The Mission of the Church As the Context of Theological Education," *Canadian Journal of Theology* 4 (October 1958): 252.

Denominational loyalty in its deepest sense is no more incompatible with ecumenical concern than family faithfulness is incompatible with community responsibility. In experience, indeed, these often appear to be in conflict, but ultimately they are not.

It is assumed that our institution will not only study but also appreciate and promote the living and dynamic elements in our denominational heritage. It is also clear that as a child and servant of the church it must necessarily be deeply involved in the mainstream of the life of the particular church which gives to it its existence and its character. But our mission is not completed when we have ministered to our own fellowship and have trained its pastors and missionaries and other Christian workers. Neither is it completed when we open the doors of our institution to students of other denominations.

One of the decisive elements in the vision which gave rise to the development of the Associated Mennonite Biblical Seminaries is the conviction that kindred denominational groups in this day need to be in conversation with each other and that together they need also to be in conversation with the larger church and the world. If there are those who would hold such a concern about communication as foreign to our heritage, we may lift up John Howard Yoder's observation that it was precisely our own spiritual forebears, the Anabaptists, who were actively involved in a kind of ecumenical conversation in their own day, as many Anabaptist writings and records of their disputations would indicate. Yoder says that alone among the churches of the Reformation, the Anabaptists refused to accept division and came back again and again to discuss. For us to ignore this aspect of our heritage or to lose this concept of Christian conversation among our own groups or with the larger Christian church would be to fail the Anabaptist vision.

To propose that our seminary should be the locus of broad Christian conversation as well as an institution loyal to its own church is not to ignore the bristling difficulties which are inherent in any attempt on the part of a denominational institution to take ecumenical responsibility seriously. It is certainly not intended to suggest easy answers to problems of organizational relationships nor a particular pattern which such conversation should take. What we are trying to say is that we believe our Mennonite fellowship has something to say to the larger church and to the world and that to maintain any real measure of health in ourselves we must be aggressively involved in saying it. Jesus said, "Whosoever would save his life shall lose it, but whosoever will lose his life for my sake and the gospel's shall save it" (Matt. 10:39).

A VISION SUMMARIZED

The picture of the seminary which emerges from what we have said is one of a community of learning which is also a community of faith. In one sense church and school here become one. Here we seek truth but here also we confess faith, and exercise faith and grow in faith so that we may become aware and humble about our limitations of knowledge on one hand, but be bold and vigorous in our proclamation of the gospel of Jesus Christ on the other.

It is a community of rigorous and creative intellectual disciplines—the intellectual center of the church's life, as Niebuhr puts it—but it is also a community of warm and fertile spiritual nurture, where the scholar is not applauded above the one who prays, nor the one who prays above the scholar, but here it is the scholar who prays.

As a biblical seminary it is a community of the Bible, where the authority of the Word is acknowledged and heeded, and where we have no higher aspiration than to become faithful servants of the Word—*Diener am Wort*, as our forebears put it. It is also the community of human understanding where persons in need may know that they are understood and loved not merely in word and in tongue but in deed and in truth.

It is the theological community where we with open minds and open Bibles think deeply on God, but it is also the witnessing community where we testify to one another and to those outside of that which Christ does for us, in order that others may know the Savior too.

Finally, it is the community of ecclesiastical loyalty where the living values of a denominational heritage are cherished, interpreted, and perpetuated, but it is also the community of ongoing Christian conversation in which there is living contact and real exchange with others with whom a basic conversation can be established. Such conversation implies not only witnessing but also listening with full confidence in the Holy Spirit who is able to give discernment and love to the end that truth shall prevail instead of error.

9 | *A biblical/theological perspective on pastoral care*

ERLAND WALTNER

M Y OWN PILGRIMAGE IN PASTORAL CARE HAS involved more than eleven years of pastoral leadership in two vastly different congregations, the first in Philadelphia, Pennsylvania, and the second in a small rural community, Mountain Lake, Minnesota; eight years of biblical teaching at Bethel College, North Newton, Kansas; and twenty-seven years of teaching and administration at Associated Mennonite Biblical Seminaries in Elkhart, Indiana. My theological training has been largely in biblical studies, especially New Testament, but my teaching and other ministries have involved me in a constant struggle to apply biblical and theological insights to pastoral life and care. During the past five years I have also become involved in thinking more focally about health care in that I serve as a part-time executive secretary for Mennonite Medical Association, which brings together more than 500 physicians in Christian fellowship in reflection on some of the bio-ethical issues and in sponsoring medical students in cross-cultural experiences of training and service.

Manifestly, I can attempt no comprehensive effort to deal with the many issues suggested by the announced subject, nor do I claim special insight on the items selected, but I welcome this opportunity to share some perspectives for stimulation, for dialogue, and for my own learning and growth together with you. My contribution must arise out of the boundary line situations in which I live and work, namely the boundary between the biblical and pastoral disciplines, and the boundary between professional caregivers and the people of faith and pain.

I am aware that significant flux characterizes the scene in contemporary pastoral care because for a time this discipline, especially among Protestants, came under a strong influence of psychology and psychotherapy, taking its operational clues from these social sciences rather than from biblical studies or theology. While this has undoubtedly

Extracts from a Notre Dame workshop on Pastoral Care, Health Care and the 21st Century, June 14, 1985.

made a positive contribution, the situation moved to the point that psychiatrist Karl A. Menninger in the early 1970s began to raise the question with Protestant ministers, *Whatever Became of Sin?*[1] The implication of his lectures…was that pastoral care givers were tending to abandon their biblical/theological birthright for perspectives which lacked ethical and spiritual depth, having traded it for a "mess of pottage" which seemed to yield a quick fix, but did not heal the deeper wounds of persons or of the society.

…If, however, I were to pursue the matter further, it might well be in the framework of what some have called a shalom biblical theology approach. *Shalom* is a Hebrew word commonly translated "peace," but which has meanings vastly larger.…

Brethren Life and Thought published a paper I had written on shalom and wholeness, presented two years earlier to the Marpeck Academy in Washington, D.C.[2] In this I sought to elaborate an observation I had made back in 1980 in a health convention setting that

> *In Jesus Christ,* SHALOM *(peace) and* SHALEM *(health, or wholeness) come together. We need no longer contrast inner peace and outer peace, peace with God and peace with others. These are not to be in a relationship of contrast, but they are part of a larger wholeness. In Jesus Christ we find that peace-making and health-making, community making and person making flow from the same deep fountain in God—the ultimate source of peace and health and our salvation. "By His stripes we are healed."*[3]

THE BIBLICAL CONCERN FOR SHALOM

The Old Testament use of shalom becomes the backdrop for the New Testament conviction that in the coming, teaching, suffering, dying, and raising up of Jesus Christ, the Messiah, shalom as wholeness has been realized and that its power and benefits may be appropriated through a faith/love relationship to Jesus Christ. In this relationship we are incorporated into the living Prince of Peace, whose shalom becomes the controlling reality of those who participate in the community of believers.… We may begin to grasp the deeper meaning of Ephesians which speaks of Jesus as "our peace/eirene/shalom" (2:14) and declares that Jesus both made peace through the cross (2:15) and preached peace (2:17), thus bringing into being a new humanity in which the hostilities that separate human beings can be overcome. When the meaning of the Greek word *eirene* is seen alongside the Hebrew word *shalom* it becomes

---

[1] Karl A. Menninger, *Whatever Became of Sin?* (New York: Hawthorne Bks., 1973).

[2] *Brethren Life and Thought* 29 (summer 1984): 145.

[3] *The Mennonite* (November 25, 1980), 689.

clear that our usual ways of thinking about peace as an absence of war represent a gross reductionism which is in dire need of correction. As Leroy Friesen, professor of peace studies at Associated Mennonite Biblical Seminaries, puts it,

> *The word shalom is too big for anything in the English language.... In contrast to our own use of the word "peace" which might mean the absence of war or some kind of inner tranquility, the biblical term is an enormously expansive and comprehensive word. Wholeness might be the best one-to-one synonym, but even that is is terribly inadequate. The word has to do with the totality of things and the relationship of all things within that totality..., with the harmony of all things, human and otherwise in God's creation, the harmony of relationships, the coming together in gentleness of that which shares participation in the creation of Yahweh.... It has to do with well-being...not only of the nonphysical. The Hebrew did not tolerate the soul-body distinction.... It included physical prosperity, material prosperity, and all that we are. Underneath this term is the assumption of a webbed inter-connected-ness of all life which resists any pulling out of some quarter such as the intellectual or the spiritual...and views us as wholes. Shalom has to do with the well-being and prosperity of the most full-blossomed possibility for all that we are. The emphasis is on the relationship of the one with the other.*
>
> *It is an awesome word. It has to do with corporateness, with sociality..., with the well-being of people and it was in the context of that corporateness that the individual experiences well-being and peace.*[4]

THE BIBLICAL CONCERN FOR HEALTH

When we turn from the grand vision of shalom with its cosmic and eschatological dimensions to the issue of human health, we discover that the particular is no less a concern of the Bible than the universal. While definitions of health are almost as hard to come by as definitions of shalom, we focus here on the physical and psychological well-being of persons which enables them to function in the context of their own personhood and community. To this observer it is striking that currently much of health care dialogue moves in the direction of seeing persons in terms of "wholeness" with a plethora of publications now appearing on what is sometimes controversially called "holistic health care."

The Bible rather obviously prizes good health, also in its physical aspects.... Moreover, the Bible freely uses sickness/health images metaphorically, applying these both to individual persons and to the covenant people as a whole....

---

[4] Transcribed from a lecture on the biblical meaning of shalom, February 21, 1982.

The emerging theology of health/sickness is quite complex and at times in dialogue within the biblical documents themselves. In one strand of thought, sickness is linked closely to human sinfulness, but to challenge that common assumption seems to be a major purpose of the book of Job.

Some Hebrew thought emphasized that God dispensed health as a gift, but only to the obedient. Sick persons thus became not only objects of charity, but also of condescension. Where sickness and disability were found, it was common to search for moral causes. Someone must have sinned, either the sick person or perchance the parents (John 9:3).

Not only did this pose heavy problems for the sick who then suffered not only from their disease, but also from the condescension of other people plus their own sense of guilt and/or hopelessness. It also brought criticism on those who practiced the healing arts. J. Jeremias has called attention to a kind of social status rating which appears in one of the tractates of the Mishnah, from which we learn that physicians in the time of Jesus and after belonged to a despised rather than an honored occupation. They were, he notes, well below the donkey drivers, even below the herdsmen and shopkeepers, just a hair above the butchers. Rabbi Judah in A.D. 150 said, "The best among the physicians is destined for Gehenna and the most seemly among the butchers is a partner of Amalek." He identified three basic accusations which were brought against practicing physicians: (1) they were soothing their patients and so keeping them from seeking God; (2) they had many lives on their consciences; (3) they were neglecting the poor and giving all their attention to the wealthy.

Jesus, however, rejected some elements in the current theology of sickness/health, especially the direct linkage between disease and personal sin (John 9). He seemed less interested in giving theological explanations of sickness and other forms of human suffering and instead responded lovingly and compassionately to the sick.... The Gospels report at least twenty-six individual healings and ten more references to "many" being healed. Jesus sees these persons as units in which body, mind, and spirit were not only interrelated, but essentially "one being." In the well-known story of the healing of the paralytic, the forgiveness of sins and the deliverance from paralysis are brought together. Physical and so-called spiritual healing at times seem to merge so that Jesus' word, "Your faith has saved you" can also be correctly rendered, "Your faith has made you well" (Luke 7:50; 8:48).

Not only did Jesus heal many sick, but he commissioned his disciples to heal the sick as well (Luke 9:2, 6; 10:9). If we take Luke's portrayal of the early church in Acts with historical seriousness, we recognize that the apostolic ministry is presented in a kind of paradigm in Acts 3:1–10 in the account of the healing of the lame man at the temple. The Apostle Paul moreover spoke of gifts of healing as *charismata* of the Spirit (1 Cor. 12:10, 28). Peter, Paul, and Philip are reported as being active in healing ministries. Healing and the forgiveness of sins continue to go together as in James 5:16, which calls for the use of confession, prayer, and oil (medicine?) in a kind of group therapy commended there. While recognizing that the New Testament records pose many problems for us with reference to the relationship between theology and medicine, our point here is that the biblical concern for physical health does not "phase out" but remains strong throughout the Scriptures.

The concern for health care, including the practice of the healing arts and the development of medical science and technology, finds a solid basis in the biblical concern for human well-being. It is not separate from the vision of shalom, but is an integral part of it.

SOME IMPLICATIONS FOR PASTORAL CARE/HEALTH CARE

I ask now what may be some implications of the recovery of a more particular shalom motif as a reshaping perspective in the conceptualizing and practice of pastoral care. I venture a few preliminary suggestions:

1. The dimension of wholeness we seek in pastoral care would be shaped by the biblical shalom vision and tradition instead of a secular nontheistic approach. This wholeness is not narrowly defined, but is multifaceted and multidimensional, essentially a gift of God, offered God's people through Jesus Christ and the presence and work of God's Holy Spirit. It would resist the many either/or approaches to reality and the divine intention, which often dichotomize or fragment our understandings of salvation. It would move toward a greater inclusiveness in which both the individual and society, both the physical and the spiritual, both the natural and the transcendent, both the temporal and the eternal are taken seriously in recognizing the context and the goals of pastoral care and counseling.

2. The recovery of a shalom motif would involve focally the wholeness of persons, which is something more than an individually shaped goal, whether shaped by the client or shaped by the counselor. This sees persons as broken or whole in a societal context. The shalom perspective would thus become a safeguard against narcissism or pure individualism, without losing the concern for the wholeness of the individual person. Self-

actualization, however, is always contextual and relational and not an isolated assumption or goal.

3.   It follows that the shalom perspective would call for a deeper and clearer grasp of the nature of divine and human love, including specifically the biblical concept of *agape*. Karl A. Menninger years ago already prodded us in this direction when he wrote, "If we can love: this is the touchstone. This is the key to all the therapeutic programs of the modern psychiatric hospital.... To our patient who cannot love, we must say by our actions that we do love him/her....'As you—and we—come to understand your life better, the warmth of love will begin to replace your present anguish and you will begin to find yourself getting well.'"[5] ...Biblical shalom does not exist without biblical agape, but both need to be rescued from superficial and often emasculated concepts.

4.   It follows that the concern for shalom also includes the wholeness of social groups such as families and/or communities of faith and mutual caring. Pastoral care then is not isolated from concern for the well-being of the group of which the individual person is a part. This at once introduces such issues as justice, fairness, and healthy mutual relationships. Specifically it would seek to deal with a troubled spouse in the context of a marriage relationship, a troubled child in the context of a nuclear family, or equivalents.

5.   Beyond family bonds, pastoral care shaped by shalom theology and ethics would be concerned about the client's faith community and would seek to understand this context as well and to work with it therapeutically so that there may be communal healing as well as personal healing. Instead of pastoral care being a one-to-one relationship, it becomes a corporate experience as suggested in such passages as 1 Corinthians 12:26: "If one member suffers, all suffer together; if one member is honored, all rejoice together." The role of the professional caregiver in this context includes some initiation and implementation of community relationships that enhance healing processes and nurture the new or the restored wholeness.

6.   While the implementation of the shalom vision may well take a variety of shapes in various faith communions, its common ground is that, with some exceptions for therapeutic reasons, it does not seek the withdrawal of the troubled person from her/his faith community, but actually works at incorporating or re-incorporating the person in family/community interaction in a positive way. Each

---

[5] Quoted in Vernon H. Neufeld, ed. *If We Can Love: The Mennonite Mental Health Story* (Newton: Faith & Life Pr., 1983), iii.

small movement in this direction may then indeed be seen as a movement toward shalom and the occasion of joy.

7.   It follows also that the concerns of pastoral care will not be fulfilled with inward integration but will also move out toward economic and social wholeness. Here the concerns for liberation and for justice in human relationships become appropriate agenda also for pastoral care. This introduces a whole range of contemporary issues such as the relationships of women and men in the society and in the church; the issues of racism, ageism, as well as employment, housing, and human freedom come into view. This does not mean that pastoral care is transmuted into some form of social or political activism, but it does mean that whatever the source and nature of human woundedness that serves as a barrier to shalom or functions as anti-shalom becomes a concern.

8.   One specific expression of this shalom approach to pastoral care has to do with the national preoccupation with militarism as seen not only by Mennonites and other so-called peace churches, but now also by the National Conference of Catholic Bishops in their pastoral statements.... A shalom biblical theology/ethic would affirm the propriety of such concerns as a dimension of pastoral care. It is not insignificant that various groups of persons in the helping professions have subgroups that identify specifically with issues of this kind and see this identification as appropriate and not extraneous to their professional roles. Indeed, given the realities of the potential for nuclear annihilation and the disposition to increase these capabilities still further, the issue of any kind of pastoral care in the twenty-first century is far from something to be taken for granted.

Moreover, it means that bio-ethical issues surrounding the beginning of life (abortion, in-vitro fertilization, etc.) as well as those involving the prolongation of life (organ transplants, definitions of death, death with dignity versus undue prolongation of suffering) likewise belong to the struggles of pastoral care. When shalom as wholeness becomes an illuminating motif, human life and death are redefined in Judeo-Christian perspectives instead of nontheistic or purely humanistic ones. Then it becomes possible for pastor, physician, and patient to begin to avoid the illusion of physical immortality and to confront human death as a "last enemy to be overcome" in the presence of an eternal hope. Death begins to be seen as having its place also in the divine scheme of shalom.

9.   Finally this means that a shalom perspective involves a worldview, a cosmic perception, in which life on earth is seen in an eternal and

transcendent perspective. In this perspective, the meaning of human life is then no longer constricted to some kind of "self-realization," but instead it identifies with participation in the coming of God's shalom, or God's kingdom as it is commonly called in the New Testament. This kingdom is both present and future, realized and eschatological, "here and now" and "not yet." It is part of that for which the whole creation groans, as Paul speaks of it, with the observation that in the presence of this we are saved (made alive and whole) by hope (Rom. 8:24). Meanwhile, we live in awareness that nothing in human experience is able to "separate us" from the love of God, which we experience in Jesus Christ our Lord (Rom. 8:35–39).

CONCLUSION

In conclusion, then, my perspective is that the shalom biblical theology approach to pastoral care calls for a new sense of contextualization with both natural and transcendent dimensions, both temporal and eternal aspects, as we live out and help others to live out faith, love, and hope. In short, it is joining hands with each other and the people with whom we serve to move toward the realization of the prayer Jesus taught us to pray, "Thy kingdom come, thy will be done on earth as it is in heaven."

Instead of banishing God-talk, except when such talk does not contribute toward wholeness and healing, we would be set free again to speak of God. Instead of ignoring the human reality of sin, we would be set free to speak again of forgiveness and reconciliation. Instead of dichotomizing the personal and the political dimensions of God's intentions, we would be set free to think and talk of the larger wholeness which is at the heart of our liberation and our salvation. In a special sense, shalom theology is not liberation theology, yet it liberates. Likewise it is not simply peace theology, but it seeks peace. It is not wellness theology, yet it promotes health in all its true dimensions. It is not mainly pastoral theology, but it encourages, shapes, and nurtures Christian pastoral care.

10 | *Where do we go from here?*

ERLAND WALTNER

S EVERAL YEARS AGO, MY MOTHER, WELL INTO HER NINETY-first year, needed to be hospitalized because she could no longer swallow. Careful diagnostic tests turned up no clear medical problem, and the issue became whether to continue to force-feed her. The physician in charge sensitively outlined the problem and the options. The regimen of involuntary feeding, so obviously contrary to mother's desires, could prolong her life for weeks, months, or years. However, she would experience a minimal quality of life during a prolonged process of dying. As a family, we came to the painful consensus that we would not favor feeding mother against her will. So we had the feeding tube removed. However, instead of mother dying quickly, she began to rally and was given back to us for another eighteen months. At almost ninety-three, she died with dignity.

Father lived on several more years, blind but uncomplaining. He was ninety-seven when my brother telephoned to say that father was failing rapidly and that the nursing home attendants were asking whether we wanted him to return to the hospital, where more resuscitative technology would be available. Knowing that father could still communicate, I inquired whether they had asked him if he wanted to go to the hospital. His response to this option was an emphatic no. After checking with his physician and the nursing staff, we once again agreed to honor father's expressed preference. His death in the nursing home came very soon and mercifully.

The death of our beloved parents, both in Christian faith, included for us an experience we had not really anticipated. We were called on to participate in some ethical decisions concerning their health care in their final moments. Like so many others, we later asked, Did we do the right thing? We still think we did.

This chapter is reprinted with permission of the publisher from *Medical Human Choices: A Christian Perspective*, ed. John Rogers (Scottdale: Herald Pr., 1988), 143–51.

RESPONDING TO MEDICAL ETHICS

The preceding chapters have given us an introductory framework for thinking about and discussing from Christian perspectives some aspects of medical ethics. These have been identified by actual cases and by commentary. They have helped us understand something of the nature of the ethical dilemmas related to medical care, where several options may be possible and reasonable yet one has to choose. They have illustrated for us some of the deep complexities in the decision-making processes, some of which develop in critical moments and some of which stretch out over considerable time. They have indicated to us that life-and-death issues involved profound theological and ethical premises, which may be quite clear and explicit for some but which may be unexamined by others. They made us aware that the province of medical ethics in some sense belongs to the whole people of God, not only to health care professionals. They have nudged us in the direction of more congregational involvement in discussing these issues and in helping with ethical decision-making processes. They have given concrete handles to work on these matters.

We can respond in a number of ways. We may be quite overwhelmed by the difficulty and the complexity posed by the array of issues. Feeling bewildered, we may want to withdraw to the familiar posture of letting the health professionals decide—either the doctor "who knows best" or the medical ethics committees now available in some hospitals. However, as we have seen, the locus for decision-making is gradually being shifted and broadened beyond the professionals.

We may respond with some measure of anger, protesting that surely the Bible must have clearer answers to all these questions than we have been given. We may feel that *someone* has let us down and that *someone* needs to get on the ball and figure out the right answers. This scapegoating will not work either, because for many of these issues there are no agreed-upon right answers.

Some very few of us may think that we have already learned so much about medical ethics that we may want to express our views on every ethical issue our friends are struggling with. The truth is that this book only scratches the surface. We must consider still more questions than have been raised here, and every new advance of medical technology tends to introduce still more.

Having experienced this introduction, now we may want to go on to learn still more, to understand better, and to begin to identify and appropriate personally, congregationally, and institutionally the implications of what we have learned. In short, we really want to learn how to discern between what leads to life and what leads to death in the more than physical sense of both terms.

In any case, we should see this book as a sign pointing the way toward further exploration and not as an answer book to difficult ethical questions.

SOME EMERGING POSTURES

Written by a variety of persons representing various disciplines and different experiences, it is noteworthy that some broad lines of agreement do emerge. In the case of these chapters, all writers begin with premises arising out of Christian faith, which is not the case when one examines the larger body of literature on medical ethics. Some approaches to life do not assume a Christian view of person, of life beyond human death, or of one who is Lord over life and death (Rom. 14:9).

Basically, the writers agree that ethical decision-making is complex and cannot be satisfied with glib answers. The approach is humility and searching rather than proclamation and pontification.

They agree that the advance of medical technology is a major factor in the current dilemmas. They do not bemoan these advances as tragedy but recognize them as given reality. No one whines for some "good old days" before the benefits of modern medical technology were available.

They also agree that in the use of medical technology we encounter a major cost factor. High tech generally means high cost. This appears to be a growing problem rather than one that is becoming more manageable. Once the doctor could say firmly, "We have done all we can do." Now, with vastly enlarged medical knowledge and technical resources, the doctor can rarely speak in such final terms. This, in turn, leads to inflated expectations from patients and their families. Perceived medical possibilities are translated into "infinite need." However, medical resources remain finite, though not fixed. Thus the stewardship of medical technology becomes a critical issue.

The writers identify the issue of *Who decides?* as fundamental. For a time, the physician in charge was the ultimate decision-maker. He or she received this power from the patient, the family, the insurance company, and society very broadly. Gradually this is changing, especially in that the personhood of the patient is being rediscovered. And since the patient exists in the context of family and society, medical ethics becomes more than a private negotiation between physician and patient. This immediately makes the decision-making process more complex.

The writers agree that the church has a role to play at various levels in responding to ethical dilemmas in relation to medical care. At a theological level, much more help is needed in discerning the biblical-ethical grounds for decisions. Very few of the many books written on medical ethics explore in depth the place and significance of the Bible in this process.

They also agree that congregations ought to become involved in discussions of medical ethics so that persons will be better prepared to face such issues themselves and to be more supportive to other persons in the congregation who are struggling. "If one part suffers, every part suffers with it" (1 Cor. 12:26a).

The writers indicate that in some ways the medical focus is shifting from preoccupation with treatment and cure to prevention, from centering on illness to centering on wellness. This shift has far-reaching implications for all people, not just medical professionals. This is an area in which congregations can play a very significant role in education and motivation.

ADDITIONAL AGENDA

Medical ethics is larger than the range of issues covered by the preceding chapters. A helpful, though significantly more technical, anthology that gives a broader picture is *On Moral Medicine: Theological Perspectives in Medical Ethics.*[1] Additional areas of concern and exploration include:

1. The relationship between religion and medicine, and between theology and medical ethics.
2. The specific implications of your religious tradition or heritage for the practice of medical ethics.
3. The ethics of medical professionals in their relationships to each other, to their patients, and to society.
4. The ethics of prayer and faith healing; the boundary between faith claims and fraud.
5. The ethics of patient care, responding to the less obvious forms of pain and impoverishment.
6. The ethics of contraception and abortion, including the issue of when human life begins and what kinds of rights this implies.
7. The ethics of various types of psychiatric treatment—chemical, analytic, and surgical.
8. The ethics of medical ministry to the disabled.
9. The ethics of medical experimentation using animal and human subjects to increase medical knowledge.

---

[1] Stephen E. Lammers and Allen Verhey, *On Moral Medicine: Theological Perspectives in Medical Ethics* (Grand Rapids: Eerdmans, 1987).

10. The ethics of medical entrepreneurship and various kinds of socialized medicine.
11. The ethics of medical insurance, malpractice insurance, and malpractice lawsuits brought by patients and their families.
12. The response to persons with Acquired Immune Deficiency Syndrome (AIDS), including both health care and implications for lifestyle.

POSSIBLE NEXT STEPS

1. This massive field calls for a new kind of biblical-ethical scholar who is competently conversant with the field of scientific medicine and competent in biblical-ethical studies. We will need a cadre of scholars who can provide further leadership in carrying forward such discussions as have been introduced above. Such persons might already be involved in biblical-ethical studies but now need to become more competent in the basics of scientific medicine. On the other hand, persons involved in the practice of teaching of medicine now may need to enter more deeply into formal biblical-ethical studies.

2. We need to develop settings and processes for discussing some of the issues identified in this book. Leadership in such discussions, whether in church-school classes or special-interest groups, may well be shared by medical professionals (physicians, nurses, clinics or hospital staff, etc.) and pastors, pastoral counselors, chaplains, or other theologically oriented persons. This book may serve as an introductory text; but many other resources, some of which appear in the bibliography, can be pursued fruitfully. Such discussions must provide ample opportunity for participants to express their own questions, anxieties, hopes, and intentions. Such group experiences should aim to inform, to motivate, and (where appropriate) to implement action.

3. We may need to give more attention in our Bible schools, colleges, and seminaries to equipping future church leaders more adequately for their ministries in the areas of ethical discernment and decision-making in relation to medical concerns. Already some institutions are giving special attention to this. But since the call is to provide leadership to congregations in this area, something more than now prevails needs to emerge.

   Likewise, those who are already in church leadership will need to have these matters introduced in pastors' workshops and seminars, continuing-education programs, and supervised reading courses. Church leaders need to catch a vision of the need and develop awareness of resources in terms of personnel and literature available for medical-ethics discussion groups, which may be set up either on a congregational, institutional, or community level.

4.   Additional special forums with interdisciplinary participation ought to be planned at conference and institutional levels to probe much more deeply these profound issues: What is life? What is death? What is health? What is illness? What is healing? What is deliverance? What is humanness and what are its boundaries? These questions need to be looked at again, not only in the presence of the medical ethics issues that have been raised, but also from the perspective of the biblical meaning of shalom, salvation, discipleship, and caring community. Eventually such forums should lead to a clarified methodology as to how physician and pastor, their medical teams and their pastoral associates, can work together in health concerns and in medical ethics decision-making to help people respond to life-and-death issues with hope, courage, and joy rather than timidity and anxiety.

5.   A reexamination of our worship and preaching patterns in the life of local congregations may also be called for. Granger Westberg has suggested that the Sunday morning worship ought to be a congregation's healthiest moment of the week. But if that is to become true, we may need to ask how healthy and healing our worship services really are. Do our congregational worship and our preaching ministries help people to choose between life and death in the fullest sense? Do they motivate persons to move toward God's intended health and wholeness for their lives? Are we enabling broken, distressed, or diseased persons facing the realities of life and death to commune with the one who is our ultimate health and salvation?

6.   We will want to examine our congregational curriculum and other educational activities to see what place life-and-death issues currently have in what our children, youth, and younger and older adults are studying. Because the issues of life and death go to the very core of our existence, it will not be satisfactory to leave education in ethical issues to our public schools. While we can appreciate and support much that our public schools may be doing within the boundaries of a pluralistic society, it will no longer do to have our children learn about sex and AIDS in the public arena only. Neither are Christian parents alone generally able to handle such volatile issues in their homes. Here the congregation, through a network of informed and concerned parents, has an opportunity to lay solid foundations for ethical living and decision-making.

7. Many congregations may see the need for setting up a congregational health concerns council. Such a council can become the local coordinating agency for health education, promoting discussions on medical ethics, ministries to the aging, ministries to the disabled and their families, or for any group or activity where health or wellness becomes a focal concern.

WHERE DO WE GO FROM HERE?

Individually, we can begin at once to face our own health needs and to strengthen a lifestyle of wellness.... We can get in touch with our own aging process, begin to see life more holistically, and seek to make the right choices for life in all of its fullness as God intended (John 10:10).

Congregationally, we can begin modestly to help our people become aware of the issues and the resources available to work through those issues. We may encourage our church leaders to bring into being the kind of settings and structures that will make continuing discussion of medical issues possible and fruitful.

Institutionally, depending on what type of institutions we are part of, we will examine ourselves to see in what ways our purposes are congruent with a Christian approach to life-and-death issues and to establish structures and processes that can be responsive.

God is surely manifest and active in the Christian concern to find a way through current medical ethics issues. This is obviously not the only item on the agenda for the church today. Yet because it is so deeply personal and paramount, because it is so relevant to all segments of congregational life, and because it is so inextricably bound up with the meaning and implications of the biblical gospel—for these reasons, we may hope that our wrestling with medical ethics under the power and control of the Holy Spirit will help to renew our theology and ethics and our experience of God's life-giving and healing presence among us as the people of God.

Let us allow God's Spirit to inspire us concerning the next steps we may take individually, congregationally, and institutionally. Let us learn to pray about these matters and allow God to begin to act out life rather than death in us and through us.

11 | *From road to river spirituality*

A S I WRITE THIS, I AM SEVENTY-NINE, BASICALLY
retired from fifty-five years of ministry with the General
Conference Mennonite Church, gradually losing my eyesight
because of macular degeneration, yet still actively involved in a part time
role at Associated Mennonite Biblical Seminary in Elkhart, Indiana.

Sixty-five years ago I first confessed my faith in Jesus Christ, was
baptized into the Salem Mennonite Church at Freeman, South Dakota,
claimed forgiveness for sins. I began reading the Bible avidly as a
teenager and began to struggle with a sense of call from God to enter
some kind of "full-time Christian service," as we called it then. I pursued
what I now call a spirituality of direction or guidance. I sincerely wanted
to know God's will for my life. Until then, I had been inclined to seek
God primarily when I was in some kind of trouble, as when my younger
brother was near death with pneumonia.

Since then I have traveled many roads serving as pastor, college
Bible teacher, visiting biblical preacher, and later as seminary teacher
and administrator. My activities log includes literally thousands of
sermons and even more classroom hours, not to mention board and
committee meetings at virtually every level of organized church life.
During all these years and in all of these ministries, I have spoken often
and much, with earnestness and even with passion, of God, of Jesus
Christ, and of the Holy Spirit.

During the last decade of my life, however, I have sensed that I am
again in transition in my experience of God. This has come about in part
because I have been in a conscious occupational retirement process. It
has also come because I have experienced in a new way how important
spiritual life disciplines are for me.

Such disciplines include for me especially regular times and
patterns of prayer, deliberate and structured meditative reading of

Reprinted with permission of the publisher from *Godward: Personal Stories of Grace*, ed. Ted
Koontz (Scottdale: Herald Pr., 1996), 175–80.

Scripture, keeping a spiritual life journal, and sharing monthly with a person who has consented to be a spiritual guide to me.

In this transition I am aware that for many years of my Christian life and ministry, my time with God was something like a quick stop while driving hard on a long and sometimes rough road. I have compared it to a pit stop in the Indianapolis 500 when racers stop to refuel, to check tires, to watch for possible trouble ahead before hurrying back into the fast lane as quickly as possible. God has truly been gracious in keeping me from crashing, but I now also know that I missed out on much God was eager to give me even during those busy years of congregational, conference, and institutional work. I was a hard driver, sometimes driving family and colleagues into undue stress. I called mine "a spirituality of the road."

Now I am beginning to see my relationship with God as being more like a river which helps me get from here to there, and also actually helps *carry me* along from day to day, from task to task, from one experience to the next. I am experiencing God as One who is not only daily present with me but One who is in motion, bearing me up, sustaining, renewing, enabling me.

Prayer times are now not only pit stops to refuel but also times of overwhelming gratitude, of buoyant reassurance, and of growing hope as well as times of asking, seeking, and knocking for myself or for others in intercession.

In retrospect, I wish I had experienced these aspects of prayer long ago. However, I now also confess that this kind of awareness of God calls for something I may not have been ready for earlier. It involves what Richard Rohr has called a "spirituality of subtraction," that is, a spirituality of letting go and letting God.

Much of our lives is devoted to accumulation of cognitive knowledge, of social relationships, of material holdings—but the call of God is also to the simplification of life, to letting go, to yielding up, to a detachment from what sometimes become our addictions. This the rich young ruler refused to do and thus remained very sad.

Spirituality of the river, as I now like to call it, asks for a higher kind of trusting in God than I earlier experienced when I was more inclined to cover all the bases to protect my interests. I used to have a kind of inward satisfaction about trying to keep my life under control, especially my own control. I tended to rationalize that I must be a prudent provider for my family and a responsible steward of all that God and God's people had entrusted to me. I tended to push my sense of responsibility beyond appropriate boundaries.

Spirituality of the river also calls for a deeper kind of love in which I am more ready to give up more willingly and gracefully than before things that once were important to me. This includes proper recognition of things I accomplished (by God's grace, to be sure). I was vaguely annoyed by an observation I heard long ago, that "you can do a lot of good in the world if you don't mind who gets the credit for it." Now I'm beginning to grasp more deeply what it means truly to love God with my whole being, and my neighbors, including my enemies, as myself.

This spirituality also calls for a profound hope that, even while I can no longer have what I once had, what ultimately matters in life is entirely secure in and with God. To abound in hope, when so many around me wallow in despair, strikes me as a divine calling precisely for such an ominous time as this.

Learning to be carried on and by this river is no easier than learning to swim in the first place, a skill I have never really mastered. I perceive myself as being still in an early stage of learning to let go and let God.

This formula—letting go and letting God—has two parts, not only one. Both parts require deep faith and love and hope. It is hard and even painful to let some things go. But so is it to let God be God, truly God, in my life. That seems to confront so directly the currently popular moods of self-assertiveness and self-actualization. It surely challenges the current cult of narcissism.

To be honest, then, I must say that I have only started on this part of my spiritual journey, but I am clear in my heart that this is the way I must go. To me it is exciting and reassuring that many others have found this way—the spirituality of the river—long before I came along and will find it long after I am gone.

Meanwhile I identify with the way Susan W. N. Ruach describes this "New Way of Struggling."

To struggle used to be
To grab with both hands
    and shake
    and twist
    and turn
    and push
    and shove and not give in
But wrest an answer from it all
As Jacob did a blessing.
But there is another way
To struggle with an issue, a question—
Simply to jump off
    into the abyss
    and find ourselves

> *floating*
> *falling*
> *tumbling*
> *being led*
> *slowly and gently*
> *but surely*
> *to the answers God has for us—*
> *to watch the answers unfold*
> *before our eyes and still*
> *to be part of the unfolding.*
> *But, oh! the trust necessary for this new way!*
> *Not to be always reaching out*
> *For the old hand-holds.*[1]

Cautious by nature and endowed with a large dose of critical reasoning, I find it hard to jump. However, I am learning that when it is truly God who says, "Jump," it is human folly not to let go. To hold on to privilege, advantage, and earnings seems so safe, so just, and so reasonable. But to let go yields peace and joy and wholeness beyond expectation.

Meanwhile, in the midst of a shame-troubled culture, I affirm with all my heart with the Apostle Paul, "For I am not ashamed of the gospel; it is the power of God for salvation to everyone who has faith" (Rom. 1:16).

And again, "For this gospel I was appointed a herald and an apostle and a teacher, and for this reason I suffer as I do. But I am not ashamed, for I know the one in whom I have put my trust, and I am sure that he is able to guard until that day what I have entrusted to him" (2 Tim. 1:11–12). This is the good news I am experiencing in new depth. Thanks be to God.

---

[1] In Reuben P. Job and Norman Shawchuck, *A Guide to Prayer* (Nashville: Upper Room Bks., 1983), 331–2. Used by permission of the author.

12 | *1 Peter*

F IRST PETER BECAME PERSONALLY IMPORTANT TO ME
while I was still a seminary student. I was yearning to be both a
nonresisting Christian (my Mennonite ethical heritage) and an
evangelical believer, taking with full seriousness the whole Bible and
especially Christ's saving work on the cross. For me, these strands come
together in 1 Peter 2:21–25. There I saw Jesus Christ both as the Supreme
Pattern of nonretaliating love and as the Redeemer, dying on the cross
for human sin and thus making our salvation possible.

First Peter was also one of the first books I taught in seminary, in
1954 during a joint summer school session of Goshen College Biblical
Seminary (Goshen, Ind.) and Mennonite Biblical Seminary (Chicago)....

When identifying *kērugma* (the preached Word) and *didachē* (the
taught Word) in the New Testament (NT) was in vogue, I assigned
students to distinguish between these two elements in 1 Peter. The
results led to the verdict that the two cannot be separated in this epistle.
This deepened my own sense of wholeness in Scripture, between faith
and life, between ethics and theology, between proclamation and
paraenesis (moral instruction). In reading and interpreting Scripture, I
have moved away from an either-or analytic approach (the truth must be
either this or that), and toward more of a both-and approach (truth,
paradoxically, may have more than one dimension). While open to deal
with historical critical issues, I have followed a hermeneutic of trust
more frequently than a hermeneutic of suspicion. In short, I have tried to
let the texts speak for themselves.

During four decades of teaching 1 Peter, I have not tired of listening
to the texts. I continue to be fascinated, intrigued, inspired, challenged,
and confronted by the word of the living God which meets me there.
That word is amazingly inclusive and relevant, both theologically and
ethically. It puts accents on—
  • hope, transformed lifestyle, and Christian community;

These excerpts from Erland Waltner's Believers Church Bible Commentary on 1 Peter are
reprinted with permission of the publisher from *1–2 Peter, Jude* (Scottdale, Waterloo: Herald
Pr., 1999), 15–16, 21–2, 54–5, 171–2.

- witness through appropriate subordination and word;
- constructive nonretaliating response to suffering injustice; and
- a strong concern about leading and following in the church.

This letter touches some of the most controversial and most promising and challenging items in contemporary Christian discourse

THE CENTRAL MESSAGE OF 1 PETER

The writer of 1 Peter seeks to apply the teaching of Jesus on loving the enemy to the life situation of the scattered Christians of Asia Minor, coping with a hostile environment. The letter encourages and empowers them to live and bear witness as Christians. They are under suspicion, falsely accused, and sometimes abused both psychologically and physically. Discouragement and hopelessness tempt them. The believers themselves and others tend to regard them as powerless and helpless in the Greco-Roman society of which they are a part.

The word of Peter is that these Christian believers, though aliens and strangers, are indeed the people of God, chosen by God, graced by God, given dignity, strength, and destiny, and born anew to a living hope. They are, therefore, called to live in holy obedience toward God and in love toward one another. They are to be a worshiping and serving people who face their experiences of suffering (1) in the light of how Christ has faced and triumphed in suffering, and (2) in the light of the coming judgment of God, which will be impartial, just, and vindicating.

Peter instructs them to accept and respect all persons and human social structures, even though sin has corrupted them. This, however, does not mean simply settling for the status quo. They are to live redemptively, following Christ and doing what is good and right in the situations and relationships that arise in a fallen and hostile world. With dignity and trust in God, they are to endure the variety of sufferings they are facing. They are to break the cycle of violence by not striking back or cursing their enemies, thus following the example of Jesus.

They are, in short, embracing the grace and enabling of God to pursue peace and keep on doing good and right. As they do so, they may possibly win some nonbelievers to Christian faith. But in any and every case they are to remain faithful to the teaching and example of their Lord Jesus Christ, through whose life, death, and resurrection they are finally saved.

As living stones, they are to be active participants in God's household, which is a stewardship of God's gifts. They are all, as pastors and people, women and men, slaves and free, to remain strong and firm in the grace of God and in their pilgrimage of faith, hope, and love. This includes resisting Satan and all forms of evil that threaten their lives and witness.

THE CELEBRATION OF CHRISTIAN HOPE AND ITS LIFE IMPACT (1 PETER 1:3–12)

Personal pastoral experience. The first Easter after the bombing of Pearl Harbor (1941) and the entry of the USA into World War II, a young pacifist pastor was serving the Bethel Mennonite Church in Mountain Lake, Minnesota. Struggling with the implications of the dark clouds of war both in Europe and in the Pacific, he sought words from God to interpret the meaning of the resurrection of Christ for that situation. Over fifty years later one of the persons present on that April 5, 1942, sent this former pastor, now retired, a summary of what she heard that day. That message served to sustain her in Christian hope not only through the war years but later as well:

> *There will be another dawn*
>
> *The day in which we live seems to be another "Good Friday" in the world. All that is good and true and pure, it seems, is being nailed to the cross. A sinister darkness has enveloped the earth, and the lights of hope are going out one after another. Men's hearts are full of fear and pessimism. And while the world is on the brink of ruin, we stand by, helpless and confused.*
>
> *How good it is to remember in this Easter Season that "on the third day Jesus rose from the dead." On the first "Good Friday" the truly Good, and True, and Pure, yes, the Son of God, was nailed to an old rugged cross. Then, too, there was darkness upon the earth while sinners scoffed and believers stood by in helpless confusion.*
>
> *On that third day there came a new Dawn to end that starless night. Death could not hold its prey. The angel's message rang out with new hope—"He lives." Tear-stained faces glowed with new hope, downcast eyes were lifted up to behold a risen Savior, brokenhearted men stood up with new courage. New life had come out of Death.*
>
> *Before there could be an Easter, however, there had to be a "Good Friday." Before there can be New Life, there must be Death. Darkness precedes the dawn. But here is the glorious Easter message: THERE WILL BE ANOTHER DAWN when the dark night is ended and the King of Righteousness shall put His enemies under His feet and shall reign forever.[1]*

---

[1] Erland Waltner, quoted in Theodora Pankratz, *Living with Fringe Benefits from Here to There* (Mountain Lake, 1993).

THE AMBIGUITY OF HUMILITY (1 PETER 5:12–14)

While Peter and other NT writers are emphatic about the importance of humility in Christian life and community, the expression of this grace is often ambiguous. Along with other Christian communities, Anabaptists have wrestled with the call to humility with considerable self-consciousness, which tends to complicate its true expression.

Theron Schlabach traces developing understandings of the nature and significance of humility in his faith tradition.[2] He shows that as the heirs of this Anabaptist tradition gradually moved way from "a theology of suffering" that prevailed during times of persecution, they moved toward "a theology of humility." Humility became a dominant theme among some of the Mennonite groups (Mennonite Church and Amish) and gave them a defining characteristic, setting them apart from "the world" and even from other faith traditions in which they saw too much pride. Gradually this theology of humility gave way to a more aggressive commitment to witness and service.

Many Christians, not only those in the believers church tradition, still view pride as a basic sin. They thus lift up humility as a defining virtue. This might lead to failure in being actively involved in dynamic Christian evangelism or in ethically oriented political witness. If so, this may be a limiting vestige, from overemphasizing a "theology of humility," as Schlabach suggests. "The quiet in the land" may be quiet about their faith in Jesus Christ and about their strongly felt convictions against injustice, abuse, and violence. If so, they have moved beyond the balance which Peter suggests between "the quiet spirit" (3:4) and giving a clear reason for one's hope (3:15) in word and in lifestyle.

…To humble oneself before God means becoming so aware of the greatness and reality of God that the self falls into its proper perspective, certainly not at the center, but infinitely worthy and precious because God is fully present and in control.

---

[2] "Humility," in *The Mennonite Encyclopedia,* ed. Cornelius J. Dyck and Dennis D. Martin (Scottdale, Waterloo: Herald Pr., 1990), 5: 400–2.

13 | *Aging as grace?*

ERLAND WALTNER

T HE APOSTLE PETER ADMONISHED CHRISTIAN HUSBANDS to relate to their wives with consideration by reminding that women and men together are "joint heirs of the grace of life" (1 Pet. 3:7b, RSV).

Discussions over the meaning of this text can easily miss Peter's high view of life as grace or "gracious gift" as the New Revised Standard Version phrases it.

This high view of human life is echoed by Ronald Hecker Cram in *Listening*, where he advocates "an understanding of *aging as grace* for the new millenium."

Cram proposes that we recognize that people are endowed with a capacity to know God and love God. They are created by and for God. Instead of valuing people for youth, for being wrinkle free, or for economic productivity, their value lies in who they are. They are seen as offspring of God, rather than as productive or beautiful from human perspectives.

Cram acknowledges that such a perspective is countercultural, perhaps even revolutionary. Current culture appropriately honors childhood and youth, and then inappropriately complains about people getting older and the impending crisis of global aging. Much of contemporary life, especially in entertainment, business, and advertising, is ordered around perspectives other than the concept that human aging is grace.

Even in the community of faith, one hears such complaints as "getting old," the burdens of caring for aging, and fears about the need for care. Many of us are inclined to apologize for our age. At times we try to keep our accumulating birthdays a secret.

The Bible is neither naive nor in denial about the aging process. Many passages point out what happens to human anatomy and vitality with the passing of years. Scripture acknowledges human mortality with

Reprinted with permission from *Mennonite Health Journal* 3 (January–March 2001): 7.

courage and dignity. The frailty and weakness of old age are well documented with integrity.

Yet something can be said in favor of Cram's crusade, which argues that all of us—young and older—would be better off seeing a full lifespan as an expression of grace to be celebrated rather than a burden to bemoan. Amos Herr recognized this long ago in the familiar hymn: "I owe the Lord a morning song of gratitude and praise, for the kind mercies he has shown in lengthening out my days."

Health care professionals, doctors, nurses, chaplains, and others minister to aging persons and, in fact, they are themselves involved in their own aging process. They too have birthdays, and eventually they retire and need to contemplate the meaning of their lives. For them—as for me at age 86—it is refreshing to see *aging as grace* rather than as *disgrace,* as a gift to be shared rather than as a reality to deny.

God is good. And even when full of struggle, life as God gives it is good. Aging is another word for being alive. Christian health care providers may do well to join Cram in his crusade for this millennium to help all of us get a more healthy perspective on the aging process as part of "the grace of life."

14 | *Embracing furious opposites*

ERLAND WALTNER

"IF WE LIVE, WE LIVE TO THE LORD, AND IF WE DIE, WE die to the Lord: so then whether we live or whether we die, we are the Lord's" (Rom. 14:8 NRSV). However we tend to read the Apostle Paul, he was able to embrace some drastically different alternatives in his experience of God. This enabled him to live with ambiguity and uncertainty about the future in ways which may be instructive for our walk in Christian faith. In writing to the Philippians he could contemplate the alternatives of continuing life or being put to death and accept God's "whatever" (Phil. 1:21).

Philip Yancey in his new book, *Reaching for the Invisible God*, wrestles courageously and helpfully with the ambiguities of life faced by Christians who believe that God was in Christ, reconciling the world to God and believers to one another.[1] He notes that Christians struggle with doubt, pain, loss, and sometimes with taunts from those who say that in a world so flawed they cannot believe in a living and redeeming God.

Yancey notes that Christian faith, which follows Jesus and Paul, must be able to embrace differences, even apparent opposites that may represent different dimensions of truth. Our faith and our life will include paradoxes in which different poles of truth remain in tension with each other.

This may include such polarities as divine sovereignty and human responsibility, divine order and humanity's freedom, God's love and God's justice, marvelous grace and the reality of sin, and many more. Yancey invokes Gilbert K. Chesterton who wrote, "Christianity got over the difficulty of combining furious opposites by keeping them both and keeping them both furious."[2] Similarly, Charles Simeon, the British

Reprinted with permission from *Mennonite Health Journal* 3 (April–June 2001): 7, 23.

[1] Philip Yancey, *Reaching for the Invisible God* (Grand Rapids: Zondervan Publishing Hse., 2000).

[2] Philip Yancey, "Living with Furious Opposites," *Christianity Today* (September 4, 2000), 70.

pastor at Cambridge, once observed, "Truth is not in the middle and not on one extreme, but in both extremes."[3]

Instead of insisting that truth must be either this or that, we would do well to note that the Bible sometimes identifies differing dimensions of truth, which we may read as opposites: *The first will be last; He who loses his life...will save it; Whoever wishes to become great among you must be your servant....*

In fact, it is by insisting on one pole of truth while excluding the other that many heresies arise. Heresy has sometimes been called, "a little bit of truth, broken off the bigger chunk of truth, that gets inflated to the point of claiming to be the whole truth." This can happen if one stresses God's justice without considering God's love, or vice versa. It can happen when one emphasizes knowledge without faith, or vice versa. This is pertinent to the continuing dialogue on the relationship of faith and science, prayer and medicine, and facts versus relationships.

Yancey has concern that we may be able to embrace a larger range of experiences in life (pain, loss and quandaries as well as deliverance, freedom and joy) without abandoning our faith in God who remains in some ways a mystery even though we know God through Jesus Christ. To cope with disappointments and disasters in human experience, we need to see another dimension of truth, which may be one of Chesterton's "furious opposites."

...It may be that some earnest followers of Jesus Christ have laid hold a bit more firmly on one dimension of truth while others have laid hold on another. For the health of the larger community, these persons need each other so that the Christian dialogue may continue as together we "reach for the invisible God" and grow in "the grace and knowledge of God."

Health care providers may also need to become more inclusive in their response to new resources and new structures in the practice of medicine and health care. It is important to recognize the polarities that develop, then seek to understand what can be learned in our dialogue with one another so that together we may move forward to more effective treatment and care.

We may ask ourselves, what are the "furious opposites" that we struggle with in medical practice today? How can health care professionals who are also Christians cultivate balanced perspectives so that they may be faithful to the different dimensions of reality they have encountered in faith and in medical practice?

---

[3] Ibid.

15 | *Boundaries of love*

W HEN I ARRIVED AT LAURELVILLE FOR THE ANNUAL
MMA/MNA Convention, I became aware that the printed
program listed a title for my presentation that was different
than the one I had prepared. The printed title read "The Limits of
Caring," and I had prepared to speak on "The Limits of Cure." While
this matter was graciously corrected, the printed title suggests another
significant experience in health care.

On the surface, we would say that there is to be no limit to caring
while we do acknowledge limits to cure. But this depends on what we
mean. In our idealism, we tend to say that our love must be
unconditional and without boundaries. Yet in practice we discover that
we actually do experience boundaries of many kinds as we seek to
express human love in our relationships and in our service.

This was experienced profoundly by Henri Nouwen when he
moved intentionally from academic life at Notre Dame, Yale, and
Harvard to the L'Arche Community in Toronto where he became part of
a caring ministry to developmentally challenged or disabled persons.
Out of this segment of his rich and discerning spiritual pilgrimage, he
writes in *The Inner Voice of Love*[1] about the need to set boundaries to your
love.

Startling as that idea may be at first, it is premised on the
observation that humans are limited in ways that God is not. God is God,
while humans are not God. And that is good.

As Nouwen observes, humans may ask for boundless love,
boundless care, and boundless giving in ways that other humans are not
able to fulfill. Caregivers may become frustrated with themselves and
their situations, sometimes assuming false guilt that they are not loving
enough, not Christian enough, and possibly in the wrong calling. What is
happening? As the patient's needs grow, so do those of the caregiver
until sometimes it is necessary to separate.

Reprinted with permission from *Mennonite Health Journal* 3 (July–September 2001): 7.
[1] Henri Nouwen, *The Inner Voice of Love* (New York: Doubleday, 1996).

Nouwen thus confesses that even as Christian caregivers we are humans; therefore, we need to learn how to set boundaries to our love.

Failure to recognize the limitations of human love, as compared to the infinite and boundless love of God, can lead either to pretense or to burnout unless our own needs are somehow also met. This is sometimes called *compassion fatigue*. Nouwen concludes, "So, in order to give more effectively and to be more self-contained in your own needs, you must learn to set boundaries to your love."

This perspective seems congruent with the Apostle Paul, who prays that the love of the Christians at Philippi may overflow more and more, but also that they may have knowledge and insight. With such gifts we may discern what is best and thus be faithful to the will of God, even when those whom we serve may not be receiving from us all the love that they may want, request, or even demand. Knowledge and skills without love will not do. But love without knowledge or discernment frustrates both the caregiver and the receiver.

While God's love is boundless and while we ever seek to learn to love as God loves, we need also remember that God is God and we are not. This is why we need to keep pointing beyond ourselves as witness to the perfect and boundless love of God in Christ Jesus our Lord.

16 | *Healing the terror within*

ET US HOLD FAST TO THE CONFESSION OF OUR HOPE
without wavering, for he who has promised is faithful" (Heb.
10:23 NRSV). Our governments and our media continue to give
major attention to what they call "the war on terrorism." But it is
important that we do not lose sight of a much deeper and more
pervasive problem which we may call "the terror within." Understanding terror as an exaggerated level of fear or anxiety, how do we
work at overcoming crippling fears in our own lives that beset us?
Examples include: the fear of the unknown or the untried; the fear of the
future or of old age; the fear of strangers or a changing neighborhood;
the fear of illness or pain; the fear of failure or loss; and the fear of death
or of being forgotten.

Not only do our inner fears take many forms, focused on many
different dimensions of life, but they also operate on many levels. Some
become so severe that they require medical or psychiatric intervention,
even among those making fervent confessions of faith. As a chaplain in
training, I remember being urged to minister to a woman who was
unusually vocal about her belief in Jesus, but terrified of undergoing a
simple diagnostic procedure in the hospital.

Perhaps this is why Scripture so often reassures us to live with
confidence and courage. "Fear not" is a repeated admonition of God's
Word even while the fear of God is enjoined in the sense of reverence for
God and for all that God has made sacred.

Invited to share reflections for a 2001 New Year's Eve service, I
remembered an old decorative rug my younger brother had given me
back in the early 1940s. Designed for a wall or small tabletop, it bears a
simple two-word message: "Trust God."

My brother Marvin was not the preacher in the family. I was. I was
the brother who was serving as pastor of Bethel Mennonite Church at
Mountain Lake, Minnesota, during those frightening World War II years.

Reprinted with permission from *Mennonite Health Journal* 4 (January–March 2002): 7.

I was the one who rode crowded trains day and night, visiting camps to encourage conscientious objectors in their alternative service.

In our family, the older brother went into the far country where he garnered an education, found a wife, and began a career in church ministries. My younger brother stayed on the family farm until he was drafted by the selective service system. A conscientious objector to war, he was sent to a civilian public service camp at Hill City, South Dakota, where he helped build a dam by day and tried to find something constructive to do on lonely evenings. He began to weave small decorative rugs, one of which I received as a gift. I have kept it for the simple reassuring message it bears.

He might have chosen another two-word message: "Remember God," "Praise God," "Love God," or "Serve God." Or he might have chosen "Trust Others," "Trust Yourself," or "Trust Fate," but he chose "Trust God." That was a message we both needed at the time, both the pastor and the farmer. And for that matter we have needed it ever since. The younger brother in camp had ministered effectively to his older brother, the pastor.

This simple message still serves to minister to us when external events of terrorism tend to trigger the terror within. The word *trust* is related to the word *truth,* reminding us that trustworthiness and truthfulness are ever so closely related. God, rather than self, rather than well-meaning others, rather than our human government, is altogether truthful and the trustworthy One whom we can trust.

Erland Waltner:
His Influence

My greatest joy
continues to be
proclamation and exposition
of the Living Word
(Jesus Christ)
as known and understood
in the Written Word
(the Bible)
and empowered by God's Spirit
to illuminate and transform,
and fulfill human life
in all of its rich blossoming dimensions

Erland Waltner

Associated Mennonite Biblical Seminary catalog
1987–1989

17 | *The grace of humility*

INGRID SCHULTZ

ALL OF US HAVE A STORY FROM OUR CHILDHOOD THAT our parents and other relatives like to tell about us. We have likely heard this story many times over, and although we may have been too young to remember the incident ourselves, after hearing it so many times it becomes a part of our memory as well.

This is the story people tell about me. One Sunday afternoon on a visit to my Oma's (grandmother's) home, our family decided to walk down to an aunt's house some distance away. I was three years old and was being carried in my father's arms. After a few blocks, my father got tired and suggested that I walk the rest of the way. As he tells it, I immediately looked him in the eyes, with my little arms securely fastened around his neck, and said, *"Erst wolltest du mir haben, jetzt kannst du mich tragen"* (First you wanted me, now you can carry me). A burst of laughter met this rapid reply, and my father relented and carried me the whole way.

As I read today's text and try to imagine the encounter between Jesus and the Syrophoenician woman, I hear the echo of laughter over the woman's rapid reply to Jesus. In this story, which is recounted in Mark's Gospel and in Matthew's, a Syrophoenician woman has come to Jesus for help. We are told in Matthew 15 that when Jesus entered the district of Tyre and Sidon, this woman immediately recognized him and started shouting, "Have mercy on me, Lord, Son of David; my daughter is tormented by a demon." The woman is not concerned with what others might think, although it is clear that the disciples are more than a little annoyed with her. They tell Jesus, "Send her away, for she keeps shouting after us." The Gentile woman's only concern is for her daughter, and it is her firm belief that Jesus will both hear and answer her. She humbly kneels at Jesus' feet and begs for his help.

Ingrid Schultz is pastor of First United Mennonite Church, Vancouver, British Columbia. This sermon is one of a series she preached early in 2002 on the virtues of the kingdom. She writes, "I dedicate this sermon to Erland Waltner with deep gratitude for his example of humility and grace."

Then comes Jesus' response, for which some put this text among the problem texts of the New Testament. Jesus tells the woman, "Let the children be fed first, for it is not fair to take the children's food and throw it to the dogs." In Jesus' day, Jews referred to Gentiles as dogs. Jesus was telling the woman that he had been sent first to the children of Israel. This was true, of course, but if I had been the woman, I think my fragile ego would have had me turn away ashamed and upset. However, amazingly, Jesus' response does not have her go away in anger and resentment. In spite of Jesus' initial response, the woman continues to exhibit faith and trust in who Jesus is and what he can do for her.

It is because of her trust and humility that the woman is not put off by Jesus' initial answer. In her humble response to Jesus, we hear traces of her humor. "Sir, even the dogs under the table eat the children's crumbs." I imagine Jesus laughing at her quick reply, just as my father laughed at mine. Like my father, Jesus also relented. Because of the woman's humility, gutsy perseverance, and trust, Jesus answered her, "For saying that, you may go—the demon has left your daughter." In Matthew's account, Jesus says, "'Woman, great is your faith! Let it be done for you as you wish. And her daughter was healed instantly."

Menno Simons agrees with Jesus' evaluation. The Syrophoenician woman makes Menno's top ten list of Bible characters that show true faith through their humility and perseverance. What can we learn about true humility from the Syrophoenician woman's example?

First, true humility comes from knowing ourselves to be deeply loved by God in Christ Jesus. The Syrophoenician woman comes, knowing what she has seen and heard of Jesus. She has heard of his loving and compassionate response to others. She trusts Jesus will respond in a similar way to her request. Her encounter with Jesus shows anything but weak resignation or a victim mentality. Humility is not a lack of self-respect, though it is often confused with low self-esteem. It is this erroneous understanding of humility that is reflected in Canadian prime minister Jean Chrétien's recent assertion that Canadians should stop being so humble. Or consider this exhortation from a fellow pastor at a recent gathering: "I tell my congregation each Sunday that they are jewels, that God has given Mennonites something wonderful to share with the larger church and community. I believe with my whole heart that this is true, and that until Mennonites get over their low sense of self-esteem, they will not believe that God has given them something beautiful to share with the world."

True humility is based on deep gratitude for God's love for us and for all we have been given. Humility makes a right estimate of oneself. True humility is confidence in God, whereas pride is confidence in self.

The Syrophoenician woman was not a weak person, devoid of self-esteem. Her gutsy and humorous answer showed her trust in Jesus' love and in what he could and would do for her.

Second, true humility comes from attending to God. Mother Teresa said this about humility: "You learn humility only through humiliation. And you will meet humiliation all through your life. The greatest humiliation is to know that you are nothing. This you come to know when you face God in prayer." The Syrophoenician woman, as she knelt down before Jesus, knew that she was nothing. She was powerless to heal her daughter. She came begging for crumbs.

In prayer and attending to God we learn the humility spoken of in Psalm 131: "Enough for me to keep my soul tranquil and quiet like a child in its mother's arms, as content as a child that has been weaned." The psalmist through prayer has nurtured the calm confidence and quiet strength that, according to Eugene Peterson, "knows the difference between unruly arrogance and faithful aspiration, and knows how to discriminate between infantile dependency and childlike trust."[1] Like the psalmist, the Syrophoenician woman chooses to aspire and trust.

A third characteristic of true humility is the ability to laugh at oneself. The woman's response shows this ability. We sometimes take ourselves too seriously. Ryan Ahlgrim has written, "Laughing is our way to humility. Perhaps the best way to puncture pride without wounding the personality is to laugh at ourselves. Humility is very tricky—it easily turns into another form of pride. But taking ourselves less seriously can keep our humility true."[2]

I recently had a visit from a friend who is learning humility by taking herself less seriously. During her stay in Vancouver, my friend shared with me four life principles she tries to live by: First, don't assume anything. Second, always speak the truth. Third, don't regurgitate past grievances. Finally, don't take anything personally, "even if they kill you," she added, laughing.

Jesus didn't take anything personally. Even when they killed him, he said, "Father, forgive them; for they do not know what they are doing." How could Jesus do this? I believe it was through knowing himself to be deeply loved by God. It was through his intimate connection with God in prayer. And it was through his ability to laugh and eat with those on the margins, like the Syrophoenician woman. Unlike the Pharisees, Jesus did not take himself too seriously.

---

[1] Eugene Peterson, *A Long Obedience in the Same Direction* (Downers Grove: InterVarsity Pr., 1980), 151.

[2] Ryan Ahlgrim, "Laughing Our Way to Humility," *Gospel Herald* (March 7, 1995), 2.

In Philippians 2:1–11, the Apostle Paul invites the Christians of Philippi to see Jesus as their example of humility. Paul writes that fostering Jesus' kind of humility includes doing nothing out of "selfish ambition or conceit." It means considering others as better than ourselves and looking out for the interests of others. The foundation of humility is the wonderful fact that we have been saved by God's grace alone.

When I looked in my father's eyes at age 3, the response I received was grace. He carried me. Grace was what the Syrophoenician woman received as she looked to Jesus. Her daughter was healed. The fact that these responses were not the result of our merit or effort but an undeserved gift makes us humble and fills us with gratitude.

18 | *Continue in what you have learned*

JACOB W. ELIAS

PICTURE THIS SCENE: PAUL THE APOSTLE IS IN PRISON. HE is lonely, deserted by co-workers, feeling abandoned, missing his books, chilly during the long nights in his damp living space. He grieves the loss of friends and partners in the ministry. Heaviest on his heart, likely, is anxiety for the welfare of congregations and their leaders.

Perhaps you identify with these feelings of loneliness, abandonment, longing for better days. At times even God seems far away, deaf to your cries, out of reach. You may find yourselves in these words by Richard Foster on "The Prayer of the Forsaken":

Have you ever tried to pray and felt nothing, saw nothing, sensed nothing? Has it ever seemed like your prayers did no more than bounce off the ceiling and ricochet around an empty room? Have there been times when you desperately needed some word of assurance, some demonstration of divine presence, and you got nothing? Sometimes it just seems like God is hidden from us. We do everything we know. We pray. We serve. We worship. We live as faithfully as we can. And still there is nothing…nothing! It feels like we are beating on Heaven's door with bruised knuckles in the dark.[1]

Individuals at times feel disappointed and deserted, even by God. Congregations also have feelings: A body of believers sometimes loses heart. We may feel lonely, lost, listless, longing for a return to the energy and glow of former days. As we reflect on 2 Timothy 3:1–4:5, I invite us as individuals and as a congregation to identify with a battered and bruised jailbird apostle who defies the chill darkness by advocating unwavering confidence in God. Let's sit with Paul, in prison, as he reflects on his life, his sense of what God is doing, his longings for Timothy and the church.

Jacob W. Elias is professor of New Testament at Associated Mennonite Biblical Seminary in Elkhart, Indiana. This sermon is an adaptation of a sermon preached at Parkview Mennonite Church, Kokomo, Indiana, on October 21, 2001, when Jacob and Lillian Elias began an interim co-pastorate there. Jacob writes, "Because Erland used to teach the Pastoral Epistles course, I found myself drawn to submit a sermon on this 2 Timothy text."

[1] Richard Foster, *Prayer: Finding the Heart's True Home* (San Francisco: Harper Collins, 1992), 17.

At times, Paul presents himself as a model for others to follow. That happens in our passage as well. Paul appears to be saying, "Look at me! Do what I do." He writes, "Now you have observed my teaching, my conduct, my aim in life, my faith, my patience, my love, my steadfastness, my persecutions and suffering the things that happened to me in Antioch, Iconium, and Lystra. What persecutions I endured!" (3:10–11).

Some of us do not respond warmly to recitals such as these. Paul's claims may sound self-serving, and bad luck stories can get tiring. But note that Paul quickly moves to testimony about God's sustaining grace, which he has experienced in the midst of his difficult circumstances. "Yet the Lord rescued me from all of them" (3:11). Paul does not claim that believers always reap God's abundance as a reward for their faith. Nor does Paul guarantee the church a future free of opposition and persecution and conflict, all roses, no thorns. God offers "not a way out but a way through" the reverses and the problems of life, as my colleague Erick Sawatzky puts it. At 56, he is confined to a wheelchair because of Parkinson's disease. We can be assured, as individuals and congregations, that God provides not a way out but a way through.

I suggest that Paul is here challenging Timothy and the church in Timothy's care to view themselves, despite their weakness and brokenness, as models through whom God's all-sufficient grace and compassion are put on display. A missionary who formerly persecuted the church realizes God's lavish grace in a stunning encounter with Jesus Christ the risen Lord. That grace sustains him even in a dingy prison! A young and timid Timothy becomes a winsome witness to the power of God. The congregation in Ephesus, upset by dissent within and harassment from outside, is viewed as a channel of God's love in their world. Our congregation, even with its ups and its downs, is a beautiful body through which God works and through whom God longs to extend grace, peace, love, and justice into our community and world.

We might expect Paul to be languishing and despairing in prison as he faces his imminent death. Paul could be saying, "Don't look at me. I'm miserable, broken, depressed." Instead, Paul says, "I am not ashamed. I know the one in whom I have put my trust" (1:12–13). Perhaps our Mennonite modesty won't allow us to feel comfortable with how Paul draws attention to his exemplary conduct. Some of us might think it farfetched to picture our congregation as a winsome and winning demonstration of God's grace and love. The key lies in our being deeply aware that Paul points not to himself but to God. In saying, "Look at me," Paul is actually urging, "Look toward God who sustains me. The Lord rescued me" (3:11).

As a church, we are invited to view ourselves as God's treasured possession, as a people who have been and are being rescued from the forces of evil seeking a foothold. Paul reminds Timothy and the church both in Ephesus then and here in this city now that through the faith that is in Christ Jesus, God offers the gift of salvation to all. Christ's faithfulness even unto death on the cross is the ultimate and climactic demonstration of God's bottomless forgiving love. Paul has already earlier in the letter, in various ways, reminded them about Jesus: "Remember Jesus Christ, raised from the dead, descended from David— that is my gospel, for which I suffer hardship, even to the point of being chained like a criminal" (2:8–9). And Paul adds: "But the word of God is not chained" (2:9).

Paul also points to God's Word: "From childhood you have known the sacred writings that are able to instruct you for salvation through faith in Christ Jesus" (3:15). The Scriptures, Paul says, are inspired, literally "God-breathed." These sacred writings give living testimony to God's saving activity, to God's gracious offer of salvation. The sacred writings also commend recipients of God's abundant grace to a life of grateful obedience. The inspiration of God's written word does not make the Bible a twenty-first–century science textbook, nor an oil drilling manual that tells entrepreneurs where to dig, nor a how-to book for those who desire to become rich. The inspired and inspiring collection that we call the Bible prompts and inspires the obedient and grateful response of those who have been saved by God through Jesus Christ: "All scripture is inspired by God and is useful for teaching, for reproof, for correction, and for training in righteousness, so that everyone who belongs to God may be proficient, equipped for every good work" (3:16– 17). The inspiration of Scripture has less to do with what doctrines we profess than with the life we live!

When Paul says, "Look at me," he is actually urging, "Look to God who saves and sustains you." When he comes to his altar call, his call for a response, Paul highlights this Godward orientation: "In the presence of God and of Christ Jesus, who is to judge the living and the dead, and in view of his appearing and his kingdom, I solemnly urge you" (4:1). Paul implores Timothy and the congregation always to orient themselves toward God and the reign of God. And so Paul also invites, "Look at yourselves." Not only "Look at me," nor only "Look to God," but also "Look at yourselves."

Some of Paul's counsel is directed to Timothy in his role within the congregation: "Proclaim the message; be persistent whether the time is favorable or unfavorable; convince, rebuke, and encourage, with the utmost patience in teaching" (4:2). All of us are invited to hear the beckoning call of our gracious God, the God attested in Scripture, the God dramatically manifest in Jesus Christ, the God whose reign still unfolds and will climax at the time when God in Christ comes as judge.

The values of God's kingdom often conflict with the values of other kingdoms. The restorative notion of justice, compassion, and forgiveness, which is at the heart of the gospel, does not co-exist comfortably with what is often advocated in our culture: a punitive and retaliatory notion of justice, a reliance on violence as a means of redressing wrongs. In our day, shrill voices urge responses that are contrary to the gospel of Jesus Christ, the suffering, crucified, risen Lord. Paul, the prisoner for this Lord, warns: "For the time is coming when people will not put up with sound doctrine, but having itching ears, they will accumulate for themselves teachers to suit their own desires, and will turn away from listening to the truth and wander away to myths" (4:3–4).

Conflicting attitudes and interpretations of the gospel—perhaps also contradictory loyalties—can be expected in the church. They can even be welcomed as opportunities. These differences provide occasions to study the Scriptures together and pray together and engage each other openly in a spirit of mutual acceptance and love, always praying for the cleansing and empowering work of God's Spirit. That way of dealing with inevitable differences is part of the church's witness to the gospel. When a congregation, despite disagreement and pain, continues to worship together and to pray persistently for a new lease on life, that in itself is a witness to the world. And this holy persistence will also enliven a sense of urgent mission to that world which so needs the gospel. Paul's words to Timothy apply to all of us, I think: "As for you, always be sober, endure suffering, do the work of an evangelist, carry out your ministry fully" (4:5).

Dear friends in Christ, continue in what you have learned! What we have learned is not primarily a way of thinking but a way of being, a way of behaving, a way of responding to God's grace. So, even when God seems far away, keep on trusting God. Even when others in the church disappoint or hurt you, trust God, and, in trusting God, learn to trust each other more deeply. We need to do what we have learned to do from our role models, from Scripture, ultimately from God in Jesus Christ: We pray. We listen to each other. We care for each other. We worship. We carry out our routines in the present, always alert to more faithful ways of being the church. What we learned to do in the light of God's abundant love let us also do in the dark of God's seeming absence. As we continue in the hope we have learned, we will not lose heart!

19 | *Multiplying mission*

JOHN CHANCELLOR, NBC NEWS ANCHOR, SUFFERING from cancer said, "If you want to make God laugh, tell God of your plans." God laughed on the day of the feeding of the 5,000. What happened that day was not in the plans of Jesus and the disciples. That day they were seeking solitude, a retreat to contemplate John the Baptist's recent execution. They had retired to a desolate place. But instead of solitude, they found themselves in a throng! The crowds followed them there, insistent in their pleas for healing.

This was to be a day of miracles, not retreat; a day when the mission of Jesus and his disciples would be multiplied; a day when the disciples would receive a new perspective on what they possessed, and what that possession meant for the kingdom of God.

I work with the transformation of our present bodies of the Mennonite Church and the General Conference Mennonite Church into a new church. In one way, it is painstaking work, building brick by brick, proposal by proposal, relationship by relationship. In another, more profound way, it is nothing less than a miracle.

We have our own ideas and plans about this new church. But God has even greater plans than ours. God has brought us to a new day in our journey as churches. Before this day is out, God will laugh and teach us new things about our own plans and expectations. God will reveal to us the meaning of Paul's words in Ephesians 3:20—"Now to him who by the power at work within us is able to accomplish abundantly far more than all we can ask or imagine...." God will draw us together in Christ!

Transformation: It's an audacious word! It seems too big a word for humble Mennonites. But in our day it has become a watchword for opening ourselves to much greater things. Now we speak not only of sending missionaries, but of becoming a missional church. This means

James Schrag is executive director of Mennonite Church USA. This sermon was first preached on October 29, 2000, at First Mennonite Church, Newton, Kansas.

that the instinct for mission would become part of us all! That's transformation!

Before that day ended the disciples would be transformed in their understanding of their capacity for ministry. Perhaps the scene was familiar to the disciples—the throngs pressing around Jesus. Did they act as organizers, queuing people up in orderly fashion? Or did they simply stand back and watch? After all, this miracle business was about Jesus, not about them, right?

We must make similar decisions, you know. Are we only spectators to the mighty acts of God? Or are we participants?

Was it the cry of a hungry baby or the rumblings in their own stomachs that reminded the disciples that the day was drawing to a close? Now it was their turn. They made a suggestion to Jesus. Their wisdom seems on target to us: "Here we are out in the middle of nowhere," they said to the Master, "with no food to offer these people. Send them back to the villages, where they can buy food and satisfy their own hunger" (Matt. 14:15). The message is implicit: "Jesus, you have provided enough for these people today. Now it is time for them to provide for themselves!" The disciples, in effect, declared the day of miracles finished!

We also set limits—because it seems the prudent thing to do. This is particularly so among Christians who know they have additional means at their disposal. The goal of a rich congregation, I have observed, is to meet the annual budget, but never to exceed it; for if the goal is to exceed the budget, where does one call a halt? So only poor congregations can rejoice in exceeding their own expectations, for every excess to them is a miracle, a work of God in their midst!

Perhaps the disciples had an inkling that there was more in them to give. But like the rich congregation, they had learned to pace their contribution. Enough had been offered for one day, and the people must be sent away to get the rest for themselves. They approached Jesus with this logic, so familiar to us here today. But Jesus turns to his disciples and says, simply, "No, they don't need to leave. *You* feed them."

If we were reading from the Gospel according to John today, here is where the little boy with the five loaves and two fish would enter. But in Matthew's account, there is no little boy—there are only Jesus, the disciples, and the hungry crowd. The disciple's reply is revealing about the disciples, and perhaps it is revealing about us. As the NRSV put it: "We have nothing here but five loaves and two fish." Translation: "Lord, we have enough for ourselves, but not for them!" Friends, the essence of our transformation in the Mennonite church in this day will come when we realize that what we have is not just for us; it is for the world!

An old monk had planned a pilgrimage to the holy sepulcher in Jerusalem. Finally, after forty years of saving, he had enough for the journey. When he had not gone far, he came upon a pale, thin man who was digging roots in the ground.

"Good morning," the man said. "Where are you going?"

"I am going to the holy sepulcher where Christ was buried, and I am going to march around it three times and pray," the monk replied.

The man in the field said, "That trip will cost much money."

"Yes," replied the monk, "all my life savings."

"Then," the man replied, "why not march around me three times and give me the money so that my wife and children might eat."

And that is what the monk did.

God did not laugh; God wept for joy.

The admonition of Jesus sinks home: "*You* give them something to eat!" The disciples realized that what they possessed was not their own. What they did not yet realize is that if they gave what they had to Jesus, there would be another miracle—perhaps the greatest one of all!

Again, the truth strikes home to us with great force: Most of us live our lives attuned to scarcity. There are limits to what we can do. What we have can only go so far. We have adopted this view of our church too; particularly in these challenging days of change and renewal in the church, we are prone to see things in limited ways. There just isn't enough to go around—not enough wisdom in the church, not enough faithfulness, not enough leadership, not enough resources, not enough trust in our relationships to become one body together! We see the problems, not the possibilities. We sense scarcity, not abundance. We turn to logic—"Send them away; we can't do it!" We expect no miracles with the meager portions we possess!

Now we know the words of Jesus are spoken to *us*: "No, *you* feed them!" With the disciples we stand like stone, perplexed and confused, until Jesus breaks the silence: "Bring the loaves and fish to me." Either in desperation or in faith the disciples obey. They have leaped a barrier!

A certain equestrian book teaches riders of horses how to overcome their fear of jumping the horse over a tall fence. It says, "Take your heart and throw it over the fence, and then jump after it!" Now, that gives new meaning to giving your heart to Jesus, doesn't it?

Jesus receives nothing less than the hearts of the disciples, not just their supper. He looks toward heaven, breaks and blesses the loaves, and returns them to the disciples. The day ends with the greatest miracle: *The disciples* are now feeding the multitude! The blessing of Jesus has transformed their own capacity beyond their furthest imagination! Now God is not laughing, but tears of joy stream down the face of the Divine!

People ask me these days why I give myself to the work of our church's transformation. It seems too large, too audacious a task. They tell me, "I would not have your job for anything." But I am in this because I believe that if the Mennonite church will unselfishly give all it has to Jesus, he will multiply and transform this mission, and there will an abundance left over!

I close with a story of a dear friend and trusted colleague, Karl Sommers of Goshen, Indiana. Karl is a member of the Transformation Team, and a vice president with Mennonite Mutual Aid. Karl wears thick glasses. About three months ago he underwent delicate eye surgery to improve his sight. Karl traveled to a specialist in Indianapolis. He had not met the surgeon, and determined that he had only one thing to make clear to the doctor before the surgery. When he met the surgeon, right before the surgery, he pointed to his good eye. He wanted to be sure the surgeon would not make the mistake of working on his good eye!

When Karl opened his eyes after surgery he could see much better. But then he noticed the pain was in his good eye! Sure enough, that is where the surgeon had done his work. He explained that the condition of Karl's poor eye was just too delicate. He had opted to work on the good eye instead. "Your brain will make the correction," he told Karl.

Last September, Karl told that story to the Constituency Leader's Council, a gathering of conference leaders who met to grapple with troublesome membership guidelines for our new church. His experience becomes a parable for the church in these days. We are concerned about the church's vision. Naturally, we think the new church's vision can be focused if we work at areas where the vision seems dim, where there are disagreements and tensions. It is perfect logic, but that plan may cause God to laugh! For perhaps God, like Karl's surgeon, will find it best to restore our vision by changing what we think needs no improvement at all! Maybe God will repair what we think needs no fixing, the part we are satisfied with, the part we think is not broken, so we can understand the meaning of what we have, not just what we don't have!

Today God is busy multiplying our mission in this place and in the Mennonite church. God chooses how that is done; *we don't*! So it is best that we be ready to offer Christ whatever we have, as the disciples did: our sound eyes as well as our poor ones, our clearest vision as well as our clouded sight—and our meager portions—which we, till now, thought were sufficient only for ourselves.

And God, working through us, will do abundantly far more than all we can ask or imagine. To God be the glory! Amen.

20 | *Whose image?*

THIS MORNING, WE'RE GOING TO DO SOMETHING LIKE A refinishing project, only on a piece of Scripture instead of a piece of furniture. Let me explain. This Scripture text is one of those that includes a really catchy saying. In the version we're most familiar with, it reads: "Give to Caesar what is Caesar's and to God what is God's" (Matt. 22:21).

The problem with catchy statements is that we tend to pull them out of context and paint them with so many layers of our own assumptions that we can no longer see the original meaning. It's as if the grain of the wood becomes invisible.

What I want to do is strip off some of the paint. I want us to try to remove some of the assumptions we have when we come to this text, and start looking for the meaning Jesus had in mind, for what he actually said and what he didn't say.

First, we need to strip off our assumptions about government. When we come to this text, we come as participants in the American democratic system. In our experience, government is "for the people and by the people," or at least that's the theory.

We have to realize that the political setting for this text is very different. Palestine was under foreign occupation—Roman occupation—and the taxes in question were levied by the Roman emperor to pay for the occupation. It might be helpful to think how we would feel if we were Kuwaitis being asked to pay taxes to help support the Iraqi takeover of our nation. Almost all of the Jewish people resented paying taxes to the Roman government. I think most of us would also resent

Janeen Bertsche Johnson is community life minister at Associated Mennonite Biblical Seminary. Erland was her M.Div. seminar leader at AMBS for two years and has been a colleague at AMBS for the last seven years. He has also been an important mentor in ministry. From 1989 to 1995, Janeen served as pastor of Lorraine Avenue Mennonite Church, Wichita, Kansas. She gave this sermon there on October 21, 1990; her text was Matthew 22:15–22.

taxation without representation. It was in this context that Jesus was asked, "Is it lawful to pay taxes to the emperor?"

Jews were divided on what to do about the tax. There were a few Jews who wanted to be viewed favorably by the Romans and would have paid the tax without a twinge of conscience. These were the Herodians, one of the groups mentioned in this story. On the other side of the issue were the Zealots, the revolutionaries. They refused to pay any tax to the Romans and even refused to have a tax coin in their possession. Most of the common people would have been sympathetic to their position. Caught in between were the Pharisees. They resisted the tax in principle but quietly compromised in practice.

In general, it would have been considered very unpatriotic to pay the Roman tax, if you were a Jew in Jesus' day. We don't tend to see that grain in the wood without stripping off our own political experiences and our own assumptions.

Second, we need to strip off our assumptions about taxes. Our problem with taxes seems to be how high they are or what they are used for. Few of us have ethical problems with the actual currency we use.

The currency was a very real problem for the Jews. Rome required that the tax be paid with the denarius, which was a silver coin worth about twenty cents. The denarius had a picture of the emperor engraved on it with an inscription underneath that gave Caesar divine honors, something like "Caesar, Son of God." The coin thus violated two of the Jewish commandments: no other gods, and no graven images. And the Jewish law would not allow any graven image of the emperor to be brought into the temple.

Notice that Jesus did not pull out one of the coins in question. The Pharisees, however, were able to produce the denarius when Jesus asked to see one. By showing the coin inside the temple where Jesus was teaching, the Pharisees actually broke their own law.

Third, we need to strip off our assumption that the Jewish leaders wanted guidance on this issue. By producing one of the tax coins, the Pharisees made it pretty clear that they were already using them. They were not plagued with a real question of conscience. They had already decided what they would do about taxes.

Their real purpose for asking "Is it lawful to pay taxes to the emperor?" was to trap Jesus. The text says so clearly. And it was a perfect trap, or so they thought. They expected Jesus to say, "No, it is not lawful to pay taxes to Caesar." Then the Jewish religious leaders would have a concrete example to take to the Romans, clear evidence with which to accuse Jesus of being a revolutionary. On the other hand, if

Jesus said it was lawful to pay the taxes, he would lose the favor of all the people.

Fourth, we need to strip off our assumption that Jesus was giving a definitive answer to their question—an answer that will solve the issue for all Christians. The Pharisees expected to catch Jesus whichever way he answered. But Jesus did not give a straight out answer. Therefore, we need to be very wary of interpreting his comments as either a "yes" or a "no" answer. If Jesus intended to give a definitive answer to the question they asked, he could have.

Now that we have stripped off some of our assumptions, is the meaning of the text becoming any clearer? Let's do some sanding and rubbing—working with the original grain.

The key to our understanding of Jesus' answer is found in his question: "Whose head is this, and whose title?" The literal translation of this question is "Whose *image* is this, and whose inscription?" Now when Jesus used the word "image," there should have been light bulbs going on in every good Jew's mind (actually, lanterns, not light bulbs!). The word "image" (*eikon*) was used in just two ways in the Bible. It could mean the image of God, or it could mean a graven image.

Every good Jew would have thought of Genesis 1:27: "So God created humankind in his image." And they would have thought of Exodus 20:4 and hundreds of other passages warning against idols, images of anything in heaven or on earth.

When Jesus chose to use the word "image" in this setting, he was deliberately setting up a choice between the true God and Caesar, whose coin claimed that he was God.

In this context, when Jesus said, "Give to Caesar the things that are Caesar's," he meant, "Give to Caesar that which is in the image of Caesar." Unfortunately, Jesus didn't spell out what all that included.

But the more important part of the sentence is "Give to God that which is in the image of God." The clear reference is to Genesis 1:27. So what Jesus was saying was that the questioners themselves belonged to God and therefore had to give themselves wholly to God.

Understood in this way, the famous statement of Jesus about giving to Caesar what is Caesar's and to God what is God's is not the solution of a problem but the indication of a problem. Each of us is going to have to come to terms with the normal obligations of living in the world while at the same time believing that we ourselves belong to God and are indebted to God first and in all things. Caesar has rights, but God has ultimate rights. The point is that no person, government, or obligation can claim ultimate authority over our lives, for ultimate authority belongs to God alone. And none of these can be given our highest loyalty, for that also belongs to God alone. Any person or state or value to which we give more authority and loyalty than to God is an idol.

"Give to Caesar that which is Caesar's, and to God that which is God's." The meaning for us in this text is not just about taxes. This text raises the fundamental question of whether we have been freed to live as people in God's image rather than being enslaved to the images of our world.

To whom have we given our hearts? What is it that we love the most and would sacrifice for? Is it our nation or our wealth or our careers or our security? Or is it God and all of God's people?

To whom have we given our souls, our trust? Is our hope in our own efforts to save the world or in the name of the Lord who made heaven and earth?

To whom have we given our minds? What worldview shapes our thinking? Is it the viewpoint of our society, or is it the upside-down vision of God?

We give ourselves to God by loving God with all our heart, with all our soul, and with all our mind. And in giving God heart, soul, and mind, we return to God that which is the image of God.

21 | *When the children ask*

JUNE ALLIMAN YODER

O NE THING I LIKE ABOUT CHILDREN IS THEY ASK LOTS OF questions. At certain ages, questions just cascade out of the kid. Questions might be sort of unusual: What is the opposite of Saturday? Why are ducks oval? How do your teeth know which ones should grow up and which ones should grow down? Who puts the wrappers on corn? Why does Daddy's face look mad? Who puts the windows through the wall? Do you think God would laugh if I served God a foot-long hot dog? Is there a boss of the world? Why do we have to get things clean all the time?

Or questions might be more common: Are we there yet? Do I have to take a bath? Do I have to eat my vegetables? Where does God live?

Later the questions change: Is he cute? How late can I stay out? Can I have the car? Mother, are you really going to wear that? Does God still do miracles? Does God forgive really bad people?

Questions. Questions. Questions. All around us and inside us. Questions. Yes, inquiring minds want to know all sorts of things. From early in the morning—What is the weather this morning? What time is it? Are we late yet?—on through the day to the late night news—How can hurricanes cause such destruction? Is God in the weather? Are these candidates for real? Is world peace even a possibility?

Questions make you think. Sometimes they help us think new thoughts. Some education theorists say most of our learning happens through questions. So, questions are not just fun and interesting, they are pivotally important to how we come to know.

Joshua seemed to understand this concept. He had experienced a mighty act of God, and he wanted to be sure the generations to come would know about the experience.

After fleeing the pharaoh in Egypt, the children of Israel had wandered in the wilderness for forty years. Just as they were on the

June Alliman Yoder is associate professor of communication and preaching at Associated Mennonite Biblical Seminary, Elkhart, Indiana. June says, "Erland was my preaching teacher, but he also taught me how to teach preaching. I chose this sermon because he taught me the importance of asking questions."

brink of entering the promised land, Moses died. From Mt. Nebo, he had looked over the Jordan and had seen the land of Canaan, which God had promised to give to the Israelites.

After Moses' death, God charged Joshua with leading the children of Israel across the valley and through the Jordan to the Promised Land. Now this was not just a case of everyone packing their bags, loading the vans, and heading out. This was not just a case of one piano, four bicycles, twelve boxes of books, and a wheelbarrow. Not just farewell parties and new schools for the kids.

The move was a big one. There were twelve tribes, with possibly thousands in each tribe. These people had been wandering in the desert for at least an entire generation. And now the move they were about to make was to invade and occupy foreign territory. It was scary because the potential was there for them to be knocked off the map one by one as they waded through the water of the Jordan River. The story unfolds in the book of Joshua, chapters 3 and 4.

Joshua commanded them all—each tribe—to watch for the ark of the covenant. And he told them, when the ark passes by, set out and follow it. Thus they were to undertake the moving of this great crowd, these thousands of people, this multitude.

You can imagine the dusty cloud as all these people went across the valley, with the ark, the symbol of God's presence, going before and the people following. Then they reached the river. Because of lots of rain that summer, the Jordan was swollen. It was out of its banks, and it seemed like it was reaching out to meet them.

Just as the priests who carried the ark put their feet into the water, as the soles of their feet touched the water's edge, just at that moment the waters from the river stopped flowing and stood on a heap some eighteen miles away. And the people passed over on dry land. The priests with the ark of the covenant stood on the dry ground in the middle of the riverbed until everyone, the whole nation, all twelve tribes, passed over to Jericho.

Now when all the people had passed over the Jordan, Joshua asked one person from each tribe to go back to the middle of the river, pick up a stone, and take it with them to the place where they would camp that night. After the twelve brought out the stones, Joshua commanded those who carried the ark to come out of the river, and as soon as their feet hit the riverbank, the water began to flow again.

When the Israelites reached camp at Gilgal, Joshua took the twelve stones, and he set them up and said, "When your children ask their parents in time to come, 'What do these stones mean?' then you shall let your children know, 'Israel crossed over the Jordan here on dry ground.'" Thus they will "know that the hand of the LORD is mighty, and... fear the LORD your God forever" (Josh. 4:21–22, 24).

You see what Joshua was doing? He brought together this pile of rocks, this odd-looking stack of stones, so future generations would ask about them. Then the elders would have an opportunity to tell the children about the Almighty God who brought them across the Jordan on dry ground and delivered them to the Promised Land.

Joshua was creating a question. You see, if we want our children to know certain things, we must make sure they ask the right questions. The church must be about the business of creating questions that lead to important answers. Joshua's stones led to a report on the power and faithfulness of God. Too often, what we build leads our children to ask questions about sports or fashion, rather than about the nature of God or the saving acts of Jesus.

My challenge to us is to look at what we are causing to be asked. Are we creating important questions? When the children ask what is important in our lives, what will they see, and what will we say? For the children will ask! The word is not *if* the children ask, but *when* the children ask.

When the children ask you, what will they ask about? You can shape the questions. And what will you tell them your life means? What are you able to answer when the children ask?

Joshua was aware of the mighty acts of God in his life and was convinced of God's faithfulness to all generations. What do you say when the children ask?

22 | *Jesus, the Lord of all nations*

LAWRENCE H. HART

I AM ONE OF THE TRADITIONAL PEACE CHIEFS OF THE Cheyenne tribe in Oklahoma. I take this tribal role seriously. I see no conflict in this role with my Christian faith, and in fact, each gives strength to the other. But in my role as a peace chief, I am always discerning parameters for my involvement in traditional activities.

The Cheyenne people in Oklahoma conduct a special ceremony during the summer solstice. I perform two roles in the ceremony. One is as a camp crier. I am third in line. If neither the first crier nor the second crier is in camp, I am asked. In our recent ceremony, I was asked to be the crier twice. A camp crier serves as an announcer. The Cheyenne people camp in a large circle, with an opening to the east. The crier walks inside the circle, beginning from the southeast, and as he walks in that large circle, he announces loudly in the Cheyenne language the next event that is to take place. The crier makes the first announcement at the southeast part of the camp, then at the southwest, northwest, and northeast. The crier finishes facing east. Then he waits awhile. He repeats a second time, then a third, then a final time.

Before I can serve as a crier, I must undergo a ritual. A traditional person with authority will perform it. The traditionalist and I are on bare ground. I must be on my knees, physically touching the earth. As I kneel, I must hold out my arms. I must not look at what is being done immediately in front of me. So I don't look. Ever. I usually turn my face, and I shut my eyes. All I know is that the traditionalist performing the ritual spits toward my hands. Yes, spits. Not once but four times.

When I mentioned that the traditionalist spits, what was your reaction? Did you think, "Oh, that's gross!"? Did you think, "I would not participate in this ritual because it is not Christian"?

Lawrence Hart writes, "I went to Bethel College fifty years ago and took a class under Dr. Erland Waltner. After graduating from Bethel in 1961 I attended Mennonite Biblical Seminary for two years and took a preaching class under him." This message was developed for a presentation at Native Assembly 2000 in Kykotsmovi, Arizona. The assembly included Mennonite First Nations and Native American people, conference staff, seminary professors, and others.

The second task I perform in the ceremony is to help locate and cut down a special tree. The tree must be a cottonwood. It must be fairly large. It must have a straight trunk, and a fork with both limbs the same size. The fork must be at least fourteen feet above the ground. The chiefs look for such a tree. At an appropriate time during the ceremonies, some of the chiefs will leave the camp to cut down that tree. Before the tree is cut, rituals are conducted. After they cut it, they bring it to the camp. It is considered a grandfather and is used as a center pole in a huge lodge. It is the last forked pole to be raised.

When I said that the tree is considered a grandfather, how did you respond? Now, I know a tree is not human. And I can imagine an anthropologist or ethno-historian would conclude that we worship trees. Perhaps you thought, "This is surely not biblical or Christian!" "How can a Christian participate in traditional rituals that are so pagan?"

Hold your thoughts as I read from Mark 8:22–26 (TEV):

They came to Bethsaida, where some people brought a blind man to Jesus and begged him to touch him. Jesus took the blind man by the hand and led him out of the village. After spitting on the man's eyes, Jesus placed his hands on him and asked him, "Can you see anything?"

The man looked up and said: "Yes, I can see people, but they look like trees, walking around."

Jesus again placed his hands on the man's eyes. This time the man looked intently, his eyesight returned, and he saw everything clearly. Jesus then sent him home with the order, "Don't go back into the village."

We can agree that what Jesus did—spitting on the man's eyes—is not gross, much less pagan. We can also agree that what the man initially saw—trees walking—is not offensive. But when I described my cultural traditions, you may have had different reactions. When a Native traditionalist performs a ritual involving spitting, you may have a negative response that you didn't have when you heard that Jesus did the same thing. When you heard that in our ceremony we consider a tree as a person, you may have found that offensive, though you were not offended by the blind man's way of speaking in the biblical story.

What is the reason for the different reactions to similar phenomena? Howard Zehr reminds us that the lenses with which we look at something affect our perception of it.[1] They frame what we see and filter out certain aspects of it. If we change lenses, we may pick up something we had not seen before. Using a similar image, Menno Wiebe suggests

---

[1] Howard Zehr, *Changing Lenses: A New Focus for Crime and Justice* (Scottdale: Herald Pr., 1990).

that culturally we have different eyes: Some eyes are Euro-Canadian (or Euro-western), and some eyes are First Nations (or Native).

I have come to the conclusion that the Euro-western world has filtered out much of the biblical story, and with it much of who Jesus was and what he did. And I have concluded that we Native people do not read the Bible or see Jesus from our own eyes, because we read it and see him through Euro-western eyes.

When we look at Jesus, we don't perceive him as we would if our eyes or lenses were truly Native. For example, we do not see his healings as rituals like those our tribal people perform. What is a ritual? A ritual is a ceremony that consists of a task one does, in a certain manner or prescribed sequence, using certain elements. In Native rituals of healing or blessing, one needs sage or sweet grass or cedar, or some other common substance. Consider the story I read. Jesus' healing ritual involved taking the blind man by the hand and leading him away from the village. Jesus used saliva to perform the ritual. Looked at with Native eyes, this is tribal ritual.

A biblical metaphor, like a Native metaphor, can speak of people as trees: Listen to Isaiah 61:1a, 3b (NRSV): "The spirit of the Lord GOD is upon me, because the LORD has anointed me; he has sent me to bring good news to the oppressed…that they may be called oaks of righteousness." Or Psalm 1:1, 3 (NRSV): "Happy are those who do not follow the advice of the wicked…. They are like trees planted by streams of water, which yield their fruit in its season, and their leaves do not wither." The Scriptures also include metaphors of trees as people. According to 1 Chronicles 16:33 (TEV), "the trees in the woods will shout for joy before the LORD, when he comes to rule the earth."

Jesus was a tribal person, from the tribe of Judah. God chose to reveal himself through a tribal person. You wouldn't know this from watching evangelists telecasting from super church buildings. The manger at Christ's birth and the sandals on his feet when he walked the earth are far removed from television cameras in luxurious sanctuaries. Jesus, the Lord of all nations, has more in common with us Native people. He has been so westernized that we don't even recognize him as a tribal person. Admittedly, the Hebrew tribes are not exactly the same as our Native tribes. But neither are the Hebrew tribes Euro-western. And definitely, Jesus was not an Anglo.

With Native eyes, one sees many similarities between Hebrew tribal culture and that of Native peoples. Infants in Jesus' time had a naming ceremony on a certain day after their birth. Mary and Joseph observed this cultural tradition, which had become religious law. As Native people, we give an Indian name to our infants. Can we perform traditional naming ceremonies of our beloved infants in our churches? Do we want to?

Jesus knew his earthly heritage. He knew that David was an ancestor. His earthly parents, Mary and Joseph, traveled to Bethlehem before he was born, to enroll. Native people know the reserve or reservation or community within a community that we come from. We know some great ancestor from whom we are descended. We are also enrolled on a tribal roll. We know what tribe we belong to. We may not be full blood. Neither was Jesus, as we know from the beautiful story of Ruth and Naomi. It didn't matter. Jesus was still of the tribe of Judah.

After Mary and Martha lost their brother, Lazarus, family members and others hired to wail (as was customary) were there when Jesus finally arrived. Relatives and friends' expressions of grief were no different than what our people do today. Native funerals have more in common with the grieving described in the story of Lazarus than with non-Native funeral customs.

We need to come to see the biblical story as a whole, and Jesus in particular, using our own Native eyes and lenses. If we frame him from within our culture, we will enrich our lives as Native people. And we will enrich the lives of our Euro-western sisters and brothers. Iris de Leon–Hartshorn, Mennonite Central Committee U.S. director of peace and justice ministries, has written that all the different worldviews are a gift to humanity, and allowing indigenous people to live out their Christian identity through worship should be considered a gift. I offer some examples from Cheyenne people living out their Christian identity, who enhance our worship experiences.

Nearly 120 years ago, Rudolphe Petter, a linguist, came from Switzerland to our Cheyenne and Arapaho reservation. Petter studied our language and worked on translating some familiar Christian songs into Cheyenne. Language informants who had been baptized by Mennonite missionaries helped him. Their translation of "Silent night" was not literal. The Cheyenne informants were steeped in their culture; their translation reflects their high regard for the earth:

Pa vi di iv	*It was a good night*
n i xo i va	*at that time*
gi hoi inz, ho i va	*when he came to earth*
Jesus Vo sta nivs so ma ni hi	*Jesus, the Giver of Life*

This expression of the incarnation message of Christian faith through a Native culture is theologically correct. The Cheyenne translation enriches the song, and it nurtures and deepens our faith when we use it in worship. What a gift!

Other Cheyenne versions of familiar hymns translated by Petter and his informants also include references to earth that are missing in the original texts. These include translations of "Nearer, my God, to thee" and "What a friend we have in Jesus."

Many indigenous songs composed by Cheyenne Christians have the word "earth" in their texts. When our congregation sings "Ehane he'ama" (Father God, you are holy; #78 in *Hymnal: A Worship Book*), I always think that perhaps on this Sunday other Anabaptists are singing it, too, in other parts of this hemisphere. "Let your love come on down and touch your children" is a good petition. But it is incomplete. "Let your love come on down and touch your children *here on earth*" is how Harvey White Shield framed the song, as a Christian and a Native person.

During the past half-century, Native people and rural Swiss or German Mennonites have been moving away from our cultural traditions and in the direction of an increasing disregard for the earth. We need to stay connected to the earth. The psalmist reminds us: "The world and all that is in it belong to the Lord; the earth and all who live on it are his" (Ps. 24:1, TEV).

Most Native peoples have a cardinal number. For some, it is three. I think of three fires of First Nations people who live on the south side of Lake Winnipeg. For others, it is seven. I think of the concern for the seventh generation by people of the Iroquois nation. Four special mountains surround us here. The Cheyenne also have number four as the most important. I mentioned four directions, for which we have four symbols.

Chapters 4 and 5 of the book of Revelation will resonate with Native peoples who read them with Native eyes, because they refer to a whole set of significant numbers: three, four, seven, twenty-four. These verses refer to languages, elders, tribes, nations. I get all caught up when I read these chapters. There are startling references to lightning and peals of thunder. In my tribe, symbols for the southeast are lightning, rain, and hail. Symbols for the southwest are thunder and a tornado. In my tribal culture, the symbol for the northwest is four beings. John describes four living creatures. Wow! Lightning and thunder and four beings in my culture. Peals of thunder and lightning and four creatures in Revelation. I shudder, I'm so awed. The Cheyenne view those four beings as represented here on earth by four principal peace chiefs.

What else did John see on the island of Patmos? For one, a tree: "Then the angel showed me the river of the water of life, bright as crystal, flowing from the throne of God and of the Lamb through the middle of the street of the city. On either side of the river is the tree of life with its twelve kinds of fruit, producing its fruit each month; and the leaves of the tree are for the healing of the nations" (Rev. 22:1–2, TEV).

Some of our Native people go on a vision quest. John also had a vision. Caught up in the spirit, he saw heaven with myriads and myriads of people from every tongue, every tribe, and every nation. They worshiped day and night. Perhaps all the numbers John mentions—three, four, seven, twenty-four—indicate that all these people will bring their God-given cultural traditions to their worship. These chapters in the book of Revelation may be telling us that just as we use God-given cultural traditions here on earth to worship, those same God-given cultural traditions are used in heaven for worshiping the Lamb of God, the Lord of all nations. "To him who sits on the throne and to Lamb be blessing and honor and glory and might forever and ever!" (Rev. 5:13b, NRSV). Amen.

23 | *Be seated at the table*

EVERYONE LOVES A STORY. IN RECENT YEARS, STORY-
telling has again become a popular pastime. People recognize it as
an effective way to communicate a particular event or truth. Jesus
was one of the best storytellers around. He often taught using a story or
parable. Jesus' listeners must have frequently had puzzled looks on their
faces when he talked about the kingdom of heaven. To explain, Jesus
used everyday example taken from Jewish culture.

In a sentence, the kingdom of heaven is God's redeeming activity in
Christ, here and now and in the future. You remember Jesus' comparison
of the kingdom to a mustard seed. A man sowed this small seed in his
garden and it grew to be a large tree—so large that birds made nests in
its branches. So, too, the kingdom of heaven keeps growing and
expanding throughout the world. Another time, Jesus compared the
kingdom of heaven to leaven, or yeast, which a woman took and hid in
three measures of meal. Even as the leaven permeated the dough, so the
kingdom of heaven penetrates to the deepest areas of our lives.

On several occasions, Christ compared the kingdom of heaven to a
wedding feast. One of these parables is recorded in Matthew 22:1–14.
Everybody loves a wedding, as did Jesus. This story reflects Jewish
practice, in which two invitations were expected when banquets were
given. The first asked the guests to attend, and the second announced
that everything was ready. The parents made preparations, special
wedding clothing was sewn for all guests, and food was readied. Then,
when everything was finished, the groom's father sent word. "Tell those
who have been invited: Look, I have prepared my dinner, my oxen and
my fat calves have been slaughtered, and everything is ready; come to
the wedding banquet" (Matt. 22:4). From the biblical description of the
menu, it was to be a first-class steak barbecue for all guests. No mere
reception of cake, ice cream, and mints at this wedding!

Leonard Wiebe is a retired minister from North Newton, Kansas. He currently is interim
pastor at Whitestone Mennonite Church in Hesston, Kansas. He writes, "Erland has not
only been a great teacher, but he models the Christian life in such a beautiful way."

But the plans do not unfold without a hitch. The invited guests did not come. They took the invitation lightly and some began to make excuses about why they could not attend. One man had to go out to the farm and another to his place of business. The scene even became violent because of the insistence of the servants who were bringing the invitations. Hearing this, the king told the servants, "The wedding is ready, but those invited were not worthy. Go therefore into the main streets, and invite everyone you find to the wedding banquet" (Matt. 22:8–9). And they did so.

This parable gives us several important clues about the kingdom of heaven. First, there is joy in the kingdom of heaven. A wedding celebration carries with it an atmosphere of festivity. The air is filled with expectancy. Friends are invited to this special occasion. The kingdom of heaven is like that: It is joyful!

Elsewhere Jesus compared the kingdom of heaven to a marriage feast. He told a story of ten maidens who went to meet the bridegroom. Five were wise and five were foolish. In both parables, some missed the joy. The five foolish maidens were not prepared, and neither was the man who didn't wear a wedding garment. In referring to the wedding garment, surely Jesus had something more in mind than physical clothes. Likely, he was thinking of the garments of the mind and soul, referring to the inner preparation with which we approach God.

The contrast in the parable is portrayed vividly. Some will find joy in the kingdom. Others will miss the joy because they refused to become a part of this kingdom.

Joan and I were married in 1957. We spent our first summer of married life in the San Francisco area, in Berkeley. I worked at the Del Monte fruit cannery, trying to earn money so we could begin our studies at Mennonite Biblical Seminary. One weekend, we drove to Carmel. Arriving in this picturesque coastal town, we learned that the summer Bach festival was taking place. It looked like a magnificent program. We inquired about tickets and were told that there was *one* ticket left. We offered to sit in different places. Perhaps they could locate another ticket? But no, they were sold out. We were newly married, and it seemed unthinkable that one of us would attend while the other missed the concert. Finally, I suggested that Joan should attend, because she was the music major. I would wait outside. Perhaps there would be a no-show, and I would get in at the last minute. Reluctantly, she agreed. People were starting to arrive. She waited with me at the door as long as possible. It was a beautiful evening. Expectancy was in the air. But at 8:00 the doors closed, and I was left outside. I sat down on the steps, straining to hear a bit of a Brandenburg concerto. I faintly heard the musicians and the applause, but I missed the fine sound inside the hall. In my mind, I could picture the festivity, but I did not see the concert. Perhaps my experience on that occasion illustrates to some small degree the joy that will be missed by those who choose not to be part of the celebration.

A second observation one might make from this parable is that there are obstacles to becoming a part of the kingdom. In this parable, one man went to his farm and another to his business. Neither of them went on a wild fling, an immoral adventure. Neither of these activities was evil in itself. The problem was that the people gave these activities a higher priority than the kingdom of heaven. Things that keep us away from the kingdom are often not bad in themselves. They are a problem only when they come first in our lives, ahead of God. To put our own agenda as the number one priority in our lives can choke out our interest in kingdom work. We easily allow ourselves to become so busy with everyday activities that we unconsciously crowd God right out of our lives. One can get so busy making a living that one has no time or energy left to make a life. This is one of the warnings of this parable.

We have a good friend whom I will call Jim. He is a brilliant man, an electrical engineer who worked for many years for a well-known company. He could command his own salary because the company needed his skills. His wife became a devout Christian, but Jim never made faith or the church a priority. I sometimes spoke to him about this, but he never had an interest in a personal faith. One day he told me, "I have never felt that I really needed to lean on God. Actually, I think Christianity is a crutch. Whenever I face a problem, I have always been able to figure out a solution." For one reason or another, some choose not to come to the wedding feast.

A final observation is that the invitation goes out to all. Notice how much attention in this story is focused on the invitation (verses 3–10). The earlier invited guests who refused to come are the leaders of Israel who brush off God's messengers. Jesus reached out to them again and again, but only a few responded. As a result, the parable suggests that the king advised the servants to go out into the streets and alleys and invite everyone to come, so the invitation is also extended to the Gentiles—us.

Everyone is invited to come, regardless of status or race. All that is required is the wedding garment, the garment of penitence and forgiveness, the garment of humility to accept Christ as Savior, the garment of discipleship to follow the master in living out the Christian life. Jesus is constantly inviting people to come to this banquet meal.

Jesus is also urging us to invite our community, our neighbors, our work partners, and our friends to come to the wedding feast.

Years ago, I read an article by Peter Wiebe, then pastor of Hesston Mennonite Church. Peter told of a tragedy that struck his family. His 16-year-old son Kenneth had been driving home from a job. Although he was not driving fast, he lost control of the car on a gravel road. Peter learned of Kenneth's death when he was paged to the telephone just before boarding a plane to come home from a church conference in Philadelphia. As he waited for the plane take off, he looked out the window, tears flooding down his face. To think that Kenneth was dead seemed impossible. In the midst of shock and sorrow was one glimmer of hope. He knew his son had committed his life to Christ. He had identified himself with the kingdom of heaven. Peter had a sense of hope that someday he would see Kenneth again at the great wedding feast of the Lamb, when all the nations will be represented at the table and Christ will draw his bride, the church, to himself.

The banquet is ready. The door remains open, because there are still so many to be invited. God has a place for each of us at the table, and Christ is standing at the door of the banquet hall saying, "Welcome! Enter in. Whoever comes to me, I will not refuse." Come and be seated at the table.

24 | *Building bridges within the global church, turning swords into plowshares*

MESACH KRISETYA

IN SUMMER 2000, I WAS INVITED TO VISIT THE MENNONITE Central Committee–United Nations office in New York City to explore the possibility of having Mennonite World Conference and MCC–UN develop a closer relationship. We met to talk about how MWC could help MCC–UN respond more effectively to the voices and needs of people around the globe as it dealt with peace and justice issues of this fractured world.

John Rempel, the MCC–UN staff person, gave me a tour of the United Nations building and the area in which it is located. Near the UN building is a statue of a man struggling to change his sword into a plowshare, a symbol of the efforts of people around the world who seek to change destructive tools into productive ones, who are trying to change abusive power into power that makes peace and justice among people.

Across from the tall UN building is an even taller structure, the Donald Trump building, a 99-story monument to the man who owns it. On one side of the street is the statue depicting the struggle of all concerned people in the world to transform war and weapons, machine guns, guided missiles, poverty, refugeeism, financial deficits. Opposite it is a testimony to a person who is trying to prove to himself and the world that he is more powerful than the nations of the world. His economic excess is like a sword that pierces right to the heart of the poor and the unfortunate people in Africa, Asia, and elsewhere in the world. We Christians have been called to build a bridge between the poor and the rich, a task that seems almost impossible in light of the vast

Mesach Krisetya of Salatiga, Indonesia, is president of Mennonite World Conference. This sermon is adapted from his address to the Mennonite Economic Development Associates (MEDA) convention in Vancouver, British Columbia, in November 2000. He is a 1973 graduate of Associated Mennonite Biblical Seminaries and studied 1 Peter and preaching with Erland Waltner.

disparities between the few very wealthy people and millions of very poor people.

According to Isaiah 2:1–5, the peoples who are learning the ways of the Lord "will beat their swords into plowshares." When we compare a sword and a plowshare, we observe some similarities. Both are sharp, made of metal, and always need to be sharpened if they are to function optimally. The difference between the two can be seen when we look at them as symbols of status, in terms of the way they work, and in the impact of their work.

As a symbol of status, the sword is a tool of authority. It usually has the marks of hierarchy: a sword belonging to a soldier has fewer accessories than the sword of a captain or colonel. A plowshare, on the other hand, is an unadorned symbol of hard work, seen in the hands of ordinary people, literally and figuratively at the grassroots.

As an instrument of work, the sword is generally brandished in the air, above the ground, to scare off or to intimidate the enemy. The plowshare, on the other hand, works under the ground. Like salt, it does not need to be seen to have an effect. People are not able to observe the process of its work, but they can see, assess, and enjoy what it achieves (Matt. 5:13–16).

Looked at from the standpoint of the result of its work, the sword cuts things to pieces, breaking and separating things that were whole. It wounds, cripples, and kills, causing individuals, families, and communities to suffer. The sword creates disintegration. The plowshare works by cutting too. It cultivates the hard soil to make it tender and able to embrace and nourish the seeds that are planted in it. The plowshare wounds and slashes, and it even destroys some things, but it does this for the purpose of sustaining life and promoting growth.

The process of turning a sword into a plowshare is a process of becoming. More than its function changes. In the process, the sword undergoes a fundamental change. For this reason, the transformation is not instantaneous. The conversion occurs through a long process of heating, melting, beating, and being formed and molded (Isa. 2:3–4).

"Come, let us go up to the mountain of the Lord, to the house of the God of Jacob. He will teach us his ways, so that we may walk in his paths" (Isa. 2:3). The participants in this process of change were not a passive group; they were action-oriented people. The word of God became real to them. They wanted to listen, and they internalized it so they would be able to do God's will and follow God's plan.

The change Isaiah describes needs to start in the human heart. We have to be transformed first, becoming new persons, so we will be able to be agents of change, converting swords into plowshares. This change of attitude toward God enables people to realize that the highest power and authority are in the hands of God. "He will judge between nations and will settle disputes for many peoples" (Isa. 2:4a).

The process of internalization of values changes the behavior and the attitudes of participants in the process. The process of turning sword into plowshare is the consequence of changing participants' attitude and behavior toward God and their fellow human beings. The plowshare coming out of this process is not the final result. It needs to be tested for its effectiveness. The process will be measured by its end result. "Nation will not take up sword against nation, nor will they train for war anymore" (Isa. 2:4c). This verse makes clear the purpose of turning sword into plowshare: to create peace and justice.

In the era of globalization, the success of an international organization is determined on the international rather than the local level. How do we perform globally as organizations? Social justice and ethical values are becoming the measures of success.

As long as peace is not present and not able to transform all aspects of life, the process of turning swords into plowshares has to be repeated. Moreover, the purpose of transformation is that of a life that brings joy, peace, and blessing for others and for our environment. This transformation will happen only as we change, as we repent. That is theological language modern people usually don't like to use. Repentance is not simply a matter of feeling uncomfortable; it means changing the way one thinks and behaves. One who repents does not limit faith to being part of a religious institution or tradition, but sees it as a new way of life. John declares that a repentant person is born anew, and Paul describes such a person as a new creature (John 3:3; 2 Cor. 5:17).

Those who study the survival of big businesses and enterprises in the United States and Europe note that the ones that maintain institutional continuity through the years are the ones that continue to grow and develop. Their products and businesses may well shift over time; in fact, the survival of the enterprise as a whole is enabled by its capacity for change. Change is unavoidable, essential for the continuity of an institution.

Do we as Mennonite Christians have swords in our homes and in our lives? The answer, of course, is No. That is, if we define *sword* as a weapon made of metal. But as Christians we have position, program, wealth, knowledge, prestige, and authority. All of these can be swords that harm people and make them suffer. These powers can abuse other people and kill our neighbors if we do not know how to use them, or if we have not been experiencing internal change by the teaching of the Lord Jesus.

Menno Simons uses the words *sword* and *property* frequently in his writings. For Menno, *sword* refers not only to the actual weapon and the military activities associated with it, but to the authoritarian functions of government as well. This understanding of *sword* is similar to the Apostle Paul's understanding of *power* in Romans 13:4. However, Menno used it most frequently when he was speaking about the use of force and coercion. Menno used the word *property* not only with reference to real estate, chattels, and personal possessions, but also to refer to all economic privileges and every kind of material benefit. As Menno believed that the sword is a symbol of authority, he saw wealth, too, as a tool of authority and power.

Knowledge also can be a symbol of authority. When I started to learn English seriously, I picked up a small publication entitled *30 Days to a More Powerful Vocabulary*. On the first page, it said, "Your boss has more vocabulary than you." We must not forget that perhaps unconsciously we use our wealth, position, prestige, and knowledge as swords rather than as plowshares. The church is called to change all its swords into plowshares so that it will be able to achieve life and growth and produce a genuine peaceful atmosphere.

According to Menno's interpretation of the Scriptures, all genuine disciples of Jesus Christ have been spiritually regenerated, and thus have received both a new spiritual nature and a new heavenly citizenship. As citizens of this spiritual kingdom, followers of Jesus are completely separated from the love of or attachment to this world and all things in it. However, the fact is that we are still living in this world and the love of or attachment to worldly things is still in our bones and blood. We are still affluent; therefore, what we need to do now is to change our attitude toward economic wealth and to know how to use worldly things for the witness of the kingdom.

Menno said, "True Christians seek only peace and are ready to abandon land, property, livelihood and all for the sake of peace." A fellow believer's life is more important than everything one possesses. We should be ready to be robbed of all our goods for our brother's or sister's sake, remembering what Jesus gave up for us. Jesus was willing to die at the hands of his enemy rather than be the means of his enemy's death. The consequences of Menno's argument can be summarized in this manner: As Christians we should be willing to sacrifice wealth and comfort as long as others around us and elsewhere in the world are living less comfortably than we are (Isa. 53:4–6).

Without sacrifice, there is no real walking with people or going the second mile. Dealing with our social problems may eventually undo our economic system. It takes sacrifice to serve the needs of other people. This includes the sacrifice of our own pride and prejudice. We need humility. We cannot have oneness, a bridge, and a unity without humility. Pride and selfishness will destroy the union between human beings and God, between man and woman, between man and man, between north and south, between east and west.

Without sacrifice, we may remain active in the church, but be inactive in its gospel. We won't have a sense of service or inner worship (transformation). Instead, we will become immersed in outward observances and all the visible rituals of religion. But we will be neither God-centered nor economic-centered—we will be a "warship" rather than a people of worship. During riots in the last four years in Indonesia, those who were involved in the burning and looting were people who claimed to be religious. Often they did their evil deeds after they fervently prayed in their worship buildings.

Is the economic abundance God has entrusted to you a sword or a plowshare in your hands? Is your wealth and your abundance a warship or worship to God? Only you can judge what it is. If you want to build bridges within the global church, turn your sword into a plowshare. Then building bridges is possible.

25 | *How Christian is your driving?*

Y FRIEND WAS STOPPED FOR SPEEDING ON THE
Queen Elizabeth Highway in Ontario. Seeing that the
policeman had no special equipment, he asked: "Officer, do
you have radar?" The policeman said he did not. Patiently he explained
the purpose of the white lines across the highway, and that a helicopter
had monitored my friend as he passed from one white line to the other.
Then the officer informed him that the helicopter radioed down that he
was speeding. Promptly and cheerfully my friend replied, "Officer, I am
a minister of the gospel; I never argue with what comes from above."
And just as promptly and cheerfully the policeman wrote out a speeding
ticket. The penalty? My friend had to preach a sermon on safe driving in
his church.

The clever—if somewhat flippant—statement, "I never argue with
what comes from above," is worth pondering. The sixth commandment
says, You shall not kill. Mennonites often quote this. We disagree with
those who want to limit the command to murder, who say it doesn't
apply to killing in war. But if we are so sure that the sixth commandment
applies to all killing—murder, war, capital punishment, suicide,
abortion—why are we silent about the slaughter on our highways? After
all, car accidents in the U.S. take about 40,000 lives every year.

If Mennonites speak out against war, should we not also speak out
against killing on the road? Compare the number of Americans killed in
war and killed on the highways. From the American revolution through
the Vietnam war, 1,155,923 people were killed in warfare; 2,420,300
people have been killed on the highways since 1920. In other words,
1,264,377 more people died in vehicle-related accidents than in our
country's wars. However, a person dead is dead, whether killed by a
bullet, a bomb, or a speeding car. God says, Don't do it! Thou shalt not
kill!

As a seminary student, Peter J. Dyck took several of Erland Waltner's New Testament
classes. For twenty years, he served as Mennonite Central Committee's director for Europe
and North Africa and for East-West relations. Now in active retirement, he is in demand as
a storyteller in church, school, and retreat settings.

Thus we arrive at the important question: What can we do about this highway killing? I propose six things those who are in possession of a baptism certificate and a driver's license can do to prevent deaths from vehicular accidents.

Don't speed. A policeman stopped a woman for speeding. He told her she had gone twenty miles per hour over the speed limit. "Okay, so I did," she said, flashing a charming smile at the officer, "but surely that's no reason why you should talk to me as if I had robbed a bank." The policeman started telling her one gruesome story after another, of accidents he had witnessed, all the result of speeding. By the time he was finished, she realized that robbing a bank would be a lesser crime than taking a life because of speeding.

On this matter, God and the government agree. They don't always. When the government asks a young person to put on the uniform, to be a soldier and kill, we don't obey; but when it asks us all not to kill on the highways, we have no reason to disobey. It is a moral and even Christian demand.

Check your driving habits. Like so much else in life, driving becomes a habit. After my latest accident one December day in Germany, I went home and recalled every accident I had ever had. Suddenly I realized that they all had one thing in common: In each case, I had struck the other car from behind. As I pondered this sobering fact, I could almost hear a little voice saying, "Peter, you drive too close to the cars ahead of you. You're tailgating." That was forty-five years ago. I haven't rear-ended anyone since. Naming the habit, admitting it, is the first step to solving the problem.

Know yourself. Our habits and our personality are closely related. A number of personality factors predispose drivers to having accidents. Perhaps you have trouble managing anger. Anger can be a cause of accidents. Internal tensions can cause accidents. Anxiety and depression can lead to accidents.

Our driving shows whether and how much Christ has changed us. Paul said that our old nature is selfish, rebellious, stubborn, and proud, but Christ makes all things new. Perhaps not suddenly, but surely gradually we are to become more loving, caring, patient, peaceful, gentle people who exercise self-control. Don't you think having a baptism certificate ought to make a difference in our driving?

Buckle up. People give many reasons for not wearing a seatbelt. Fortunately, many states are now have seatbelt laws. The National Safety Commission estimates 12,000 lives could be saved annually if everyone buckled up.

Avoid alcohol. Statistically, 85 percent of all traffic accidents are the result of human error. The margin of error vastly increases with alcohol. We all know that alcohol and gasoline don't mix. It has taken the public a long time to rise up in protest against the slaughter on our highways by drunk drivers. Unfortunately, there is still much indifference and even objection to stiffer penalties for drunk drivers.

I have never regretted having drawn the line this side of alcohol long ago. I have also found out that it is a myth that if you don't drink, you can't be sociable. The facts about alcohol are disturbing. For example: about 10 percent of any group of people have a predisposition toward becoming alcoholics if they drink. If the potential is there for one out of ten to become an alcoholic, why take that first drink? Why?

Check your vehicle. A small but not insignificant number of car accidents, fifteen percent, are caused by faulty vehicles. In Frankfurt one Sunday afternoon, we watched a policeman walk by our MCC car. He looked at the front tires and said, "By rights I ought to give you a ticket." Then he measured the tread on the tires and proceeded to write the ticket. He did not fine me, but I was obliged to get new tires within a specified time-period. And why not? It is within our control to make sure our vehicles are as safe as possible.

In the glove compartment of our car we carry a copy of the "Lord's Prayer for Drivers," in German. Translated, it goes like this:

Our Father. *Sun, air and water belong to everyone. The street and road also belong to others, not just to me. God, you are the father also of the pedestrians and the old people, the children and the cyclists. The cadillacs and VW bugs, buses and trucks, all have rights.*

Hallowed be thy name. *Why do you get so upset? Why are you angry? Why are you using the name of the Lord in vain? And remember you can swear through the horn of your car as well as with your mouth.*

Thy kingdom come. *Show justice, kindness, respect, and consideration for others and be ready to help those in trouble. Don't be a road-hog; be a good Samaritan.*

Thy will be done. *Your will, Lord, is that there should be order in our life. That also goes for traffic on the road. To avoid chaos and to create order, there must be traffic laws, and I need to obey them. Road signs, lights, and the police are there to maintain order.*

Deliver us from evil. *The evil of speed and the demon of recklessness. The evil of alcohol. The evil of accidents, whether my fault or not. Deliver us! Dead is dead. Even having the right of way doesn't change that!*

Can we learn to drive with the mind of Christ? Jesus said, Follow me! He is our example. How does humility and service, as symbolized in the washing of feet, translate into driving? How does forgiveness, as taught by Jesus, relate to our attitude behind the wheel? Paul said Christ makes all things new. If we believe that, does it show in our driving? If Christ has changed us or is in the process of changing us, are we becoming more courteous and considerate, more helpful and patient, more yielding to the rights of others?

You may say, That's all well and good, but Jesus was perfect, and I am not. The National Safety Council (NSC) doesn't hesitate to use the word *perfect*. The NSC refers to having made a "perfect trip" and mentions making a "perfect pass." The NSC doesn't think *perfect* is too strong a term to use in connection with driving. We confuse being with doing. Of course, we are not perfect, but we can make a perfect pass.

Perfection is a process. As is true of the way we live, the way we drive is not perfect, but is it in the process of becoming more Christian? That process is in our actions and reactions; it is largely in our responses. Defensive driving is driving in such a way that accidents are prevented in spite of the actions of other people or conditions around us. Responses can be changed. We can learn. Change is possible. We can become more Christ-like even in our driving. We can learn to drive with the mind of Christ, provided we keep looking to Jesus. And remember, our children are watching us. They are learning from us long before they are eligible for their driver's license.

26 | *Christian witness in marriage*

ROSE WALTNER GRABER

TODAY WE ARE DEALING WITH ONE OF THOSE controversial Scripture passages. First Peter 3:1–7 has been used to beat on women for centuries. But that's not why it's in the Bible.

Some people read the Bible as if it had been written by Americans in the twenty-first century. But it wasn't. It was written by people long ago, in a particular situation. The Bible is our authority for word and life today, and its basic message is the same as it was then. But we need to reconsider our interpretation if we are using the Bible to beat people up. The message of God in the Bible is a message of love, and yes, that includes judgment. But basically, the word is love and a call to live in a way that is loving to God and to others.

This passage, in context, comes right after ones about government and slavery. Both deal with real life situations. Peter instructs readers to respect government but not to worship it, and to defer to masters as a matter of choice and as a witness to them. Both passages lift up the Christian as one who can choose to be a good witness. We are powerful, a moral influence on our society. We influence by our life of love—love for our neighbors and love for our enemies and oppressors.

In this context, let's look at what Peter has to say to women who are married to unbelievers. "Likewise, you wives, be submissive to your husbands, so that some, though they do not obey the word, may be won without a word by the behavior of their wives, when they see your reverent and chaste behavior."

Some of you men are cheering, "Right on! Preach it, Sister!" (It's great to have some affirmation every now and again.) I can see some women thinking, "Well, if that's what it's all about, I'm outta here!" Hang in there, and let's look more closely at this passage.

The Greco-Roman world assumed that a wife, with her entire household, would worship the gods her husband worshiped. The society

---

Rose Waltner Graber is pastor of Upper Milford Mennonite Church in Zionsville, Pennsylvania. Erland Waltner is her father and was also one of her seminary professors. This sermon text selection is fitting because her father wrote The Believers Church Bible Commentary on 1 Peter.

assumed that a household would be unified by its shared religious loyalties. Is Peter saying that wives should bow down to their husbands' gods? Should they offer incense to the household idols? It is entirely possible that this was part of a woman's role as wife. But Peter affirms that it is only "likewise" that wives are to be submissive. "Likewise" refers back to Peter's discussion of the Christian's relationship to government, and of Christian slaves' relationships to their masters, which pointed to the example of Jesus. The Christian wife is first of all to be a Christian. Her first loyalty is to Jesus, who set her free from sin and death so she could live a righteous life.

Ever since Eve, women have been trying to place their husbands in the role of God. And husbands have been eager to be in that place. Idolatry is putting anything or anybody but God in God's place. Women should not commit idolatry, any more than men should. And women need to learn to submit, just as men do. With the liberation movement, women have asserted their rights and privileges. This is not bad, except that women have a tendency when dominant to commit the same sins men do when they are dominant. The primary sin of the dominant is forgetting how to submit. We need to learn how to back down, how to let go to one another in order to live peaceably together.

So here the issue is the position of women who are married to non-Christian husbands. Should the women remain in those marriages, and if so, how are they to act? Some cults at that time encouraged women to denounce marriage and leave their husbands. That's not what our faith advocates. Rather, women are to adopt a missionary witness in relation to their husbands. They are to exhibit their faith by accepting the authority of their husbands. The Christian wife is to honor her husband. She is to do her duties as a wife in a loving manner, as a Christian slave willingly obeys an unjust master in order that the master may come to faith. This missionary strategy is simply a way to follow Jesus' example.

Peter says she is to win her husband without a word. Some studies show that women speak about 24,000 words a day, on average. Men only speak some 12,000. Now, Peter suggests that women win their husbands without speaking. Perhaps he is hoping to counter the temptation to argue, nag, or manipulate. I don't believe that he intends that a Christian woman not be open about what she is doing and why. I don't believe he is giving people an excuse not to share their faith in words. He is instead telling women not to overwhelm their husbands with their faith with an excess of words. This is too important an issue to be lost through a power play, through too much talk. So, he counsels letting actions speak for themselves, letting them whet the husband's curiosity.

ROSE WALTNER GRABER | 141
As Christians, our behavior has to change.

As Christians, our behavior has to change. We can't go on doing what we did before we came to faith. If these women had not changed in behavior when they became Christians, if they lived as they had before, their husbands would see no difference. Without words, our witness relies on the difference in our living. There has to be something about us that makes people wonder what in our lives has changed.

In Brazil, I got to know a woman named Ceca. Her husband was a bricklayer. Vado was young and virile and made good money, for a poor person. He grew up thinking it was his duty to have sex at least once a day. Being faithful to his wife was not important. Ceca knew that her children had little half-brothers and half-sisters in the neighborhood. Ceca and Vado fought all the time. They screamed and hit each other. The neighbors noticed. Then Ceca became a Christian, and she quit fighting. Vado knew she was coming to church, and he noticed that she refused to fight with him any more. The neighbors commented. Vado didn't want her to come to church any more. Ceca prayed about it. She would get the children and herself ready, and then she would ask him if they could go. When he saw that she was submissive, he let her come. Within a year, Vado also became a Christian. Before we baptized him, he agreed that he would be faithful to his wife, and not hit her anymore. Ceca's quiet witness brought her husband to faith.

I always had a hard time understanding Brazilian women's attitude about men. They really saw the sense in submission. I am a strong woman. I come from a family of strong women. I know I need to learn to bend my will to that of others, especially my husband's. However, oppression and abuse are another matter. Some women have been told that if a wife just obeys her husband's wishes, he will stop beating her and abusing her emotionally. And that's not true. One out of four women is abused physically at least once in her life. The situation of abuse is not what Peter is addressing here. He is writing about a situation where the husband determined the moral condition of his wife. But Peter gives her the power to be the moral influence in the family. Quietly, Peter is challenging the structure of the society in which those Christians lived. He is acknowledging the full humanity of the oppressed, aliens, exiles, slaves, women. He is giving them the choice to give glory to God through their loving response to oppressive situations. He is challenging them to respond in a Christ-like manner.

Peter writes further: "Let not yours be the outward adorning with braiding of hair, decoration of gold, and wearing of fine clothing. But let it be the hidden person of the heart with the imperishable jewel of a gentle and quiet spirit, which in God's sight is very precious." Peter doesn't say, "Don't wear any jewelry or fashionable clothes." But he is telling Christian women not to be ostentatious, not to spend time and money on outward appearances, because it's poor stewardship and also can be sexually provocative and therefore a distraction from spiritual things. Our focus should be on who we are and not on what we look like. I find that a liberating thought.

Peter then refers to the example of women in the Old Testament. He ends with "Let nothing terrify you." Interesting. It's scary to learn to be a person of Christ instead of a showpiece, a sex object, or a puppet. Don't be afraid. Be what Christ is teaching you to be. That is a pretty nice thought.

Then Peter addresses the husband. This was unusual for the times. Peter addresses Christian husbands, not unbelieving ones. "Likewise, live considerately with your wives, bestowing honor on the woman as the weaker sex, since you are joint heirs of the grace of life, in order that your prayers may not be hindered." "Likewise" indicates a relationship. Men also have a responsibility to the marriage relationship. Jesus affects all our relationships. To live considerately means to understand what you need to understand about living with a woman. Learn to understand what makes her tick. As some men know when a car is out of whack by listening carefully to the engine, Christian husbands should learn to know when things are not right with their wives. Learn the nuances of her demeanor to help make things right.

Honor is the next thing. A husband needs to honor his wife as a person. To refer to a woman as the "weaker vessel" is not to imply that she is of less value than a man. Rather, it refers to women's lack of power and social standing at that time. She has less power than you do, so honor her. Honor her because you are joint heirs of grace. Women are saved and under the blood of Jesus, just as men are. This is an amazing lifting up of women. Men, you and your Christian wife are both one in Christ. So honor each other.

Why should you honor her? So that your prayers may not be hindered. To pray is part of the Christian life, and your relationship with your spouse plays into this. Destructive relationships hinder your communication with God. One writer has said that men who transfer cultural notions about the superiority of men over women in Christian community lose their ability to communicate with God. I don't know that I would put it that strongly, but I do know that if a couple is fighting, their prayer life is affected. Our relationships with each other affect our relationship with God. So let's work to keep them good.

Women, honor your husbands. Learn to submit. Men, honor your wives. Learn what helps them be their best. Couples, learn to love one another, because this affects your relationship with Christ.

Erland Waltner:
His Epilogue

The work is thine, O Christ our Lord,
the cause for which we stand,
and being thine, 'twill overcome
its foes on every hand.
Yet grains of wheat, before they grow,
are buried in the earth below.
All that is old doth perish there
to form a life both new and fair.
So too are we from self and sin made free.

Through suffering thou, O Christ, didst go
unto thy throne above,
and leadest now the self-same way
those true in faith and love.
So, lead us, then, though sufferings wait,
to share thy kingdom's heavenly state.
Thy death has broken Satan's might,
and leads the faithful to the light,
eternal light, from darkness into light.

Samuel Preiswerk
tr. Julius H. Horstmann

The work is thine, O Christ

ERLAND WALTNER

G ROUNDED ON THE SUBLIME IMAGERY AND IMPORT OF John 12:23–28, the nineteenth-century hymn "The work is thine, O Christ," has inspired and shaped me through the years. More recently, I have asked myself why, in spite of its dated vocabulary and style, it still moves me so deeply.

The biblical text of John 12:27–28a takes us into the inner life of Jesus as he contemplates the end of his earthly pilgrimage and faces the cross: "Now is my soul troubled; and what shall I say? Father, save me from this hour: But for this cause came I unto this hour. Father, glorify thy name" (KJV). In a sense, this is the portrait of the Gethsemane experience of Jesus as recorded in the fourth Gospel. The hymn, in turn, identifies with that experience of our Lord.

Why does this hymn continue to resonate with my spirit and nourish my soul through the decades of life and ministry God has so graciously granted?

I first learned to sing it in German, as written in 1829 by Samuel Preiswerk: *"Die Sach ist dein, Herr Jesu Christ, die Sach, an der wir stehn..."* In my childhood, *Sach* meant more to me than "work." It meant the issue, the cause, the heart of the matter, something for which or to which one could give one's life.

I tend to dislike controversy, but looking back I see that somehow I have never been able to escape involvement in many kinds of human conflict at many levels: the modernist-fundamentalist controversies of my earlier years, the pacifist-militarist issues of the war years, the denominational-ecumenical tensions in conference relationships, and the ongoing christological discussions of more recent times. Always there has been struggle. Always there was pain. Always there were different ways of perceiving truth. Again and again I found peace in recognizing that the battle was really the Lord's and not mine. But one has to stand somewhere, so I would sing with fervor, "The work is thine, O Christ" and another great hymn, "On Christ, the solid rock, I stand; all other ground is sinking sand." In my mind this was faithful to the motto of

Menno Simons, "For no one can lay any foundation other than the one that has been laid; that foundation is Jesus Christ" (1 Cor. 3:11).

As the hymnbooks appeared in English, I learned to sing Julius Henry Horstmann's 1908 translation, "The work is thine, O Christ our Lord." Born and raised on a farm by industrious Mennonite parents and learning to find satisfaction in work, I understood that being a follower of Jesus Christ involved doing the work and service of God. We also often sang "Work for the night is coming...when man's work is done." Daily we could feel the import of that idea in our bones.

"The work" or "serving the Lord" became significant during my mid-teens when I was baptized on confession of faith in Jesus Christ. I then declared readiness to do whatever God wanted me to do with my life. My understanding of serving the Lord took on a deeper dimension as I recognized the work was really Christ's own work, amazingly and graciously entrusted to human agents. God's Spirit would be present in us to guide and empower us to participate in God's work. Whether I was sharing with a Bethel College gospel team involved in jail ministries, serving as a student pastor at Peabody, Kansas (Methodist), or Wisner, Nebraska (Mennonite), or Lower East Side Manhattan (Presbyterian), the work was Christ's.

A seminary graduate at age twenty-four, a very young pastor at Second Mennonite Church in Philadelphia, at age twenty-seven succeeding my own former pastor at Bethel Mennonite Church in Mountain Lake, Minnesota—always I was into something that was over my head, that seemed too big for me. Add to this the fact that I had traveled in Palestine and Europe in 1938 and could see and feel the war coming, and that I arrived in Mountain Lake on Pearl Harbor Day. I always seemed to have more to deal with than I could possibly manage. Feeling overwhelmed, I would sing "The work is thine, O Christ our Lord, the cause for which we stand, and being thine, 'twill overcome its foes on every hand."

Coming to a college Bible classroom at my alma mater in 1949 was no less daunting, as students began to challenge both secular and sacred traditions. Having worked through some Barthian theology and some Niebuhrian ethics and knowing that faith comes through hearing the Word rather than through clever argumentation (a skill I had enjoyed in college debate), I worked to help college students know what the Bible said so they had a clearer notion of what they were accepting or rejecting.

The call to help give leadership to Mennonite Biblical Seminary did not come because I applied for a position. But my imagination was stirred by my friendship with Harold S. Bender and by J. E. Hartzler's suggestion that the mid-1950s might be a time to again attempt inter-Mennonite theological education. The eventual outcome was the move of Mennonite Biblical Seminary from Chicago, the building of the Elkhart campus, and the cooperative venture known as Associated Mennonite Biblical Seminaries. Most people I know now think this joint venture was a good idea, but at the time many had grave misgivings. Again we sang "The work is thine, O Christ." My colleague at the time, my esteemed predecessor as president of MBS, Samuel Floyd Pannabecker, called it a real venture of faith.

The hymn embraces the idea of struggle, even suffering and death, but it is brim full of hope and anticipation of vindication. The image of the grain of wheat buried in the earth before it sprouts and becomes fruitful is well suited to the work of a seminary. A seminary is a seedbed, not a factory. The strong language of suffering is not foreign to a tradition that spawned the *Martyrs Mirror*. The promise of deliverance, "from self and sin made free," suggests the essential spiritual movement from human self-centeredness to congregational and community involvement and participation in the coming reign of God. The vocabulary of moving "from darkness into light" speaks powerfully to one who wrestles, as I do, with impaired vision.

What have I learned over the years? The hymn expresses many of the best answers I can think of.

The work is thine. The work we do in the name of Christ is really Christ's work and not ours. God is God, we are not, and that is good. Paradoxically, in our ministries we are both observers and participants. Sometimes Christ works through us in ways that surprise and amaze us. The future of that work depends more on faithfulness than on brilliance, more on discerning the will and way of God than on cleverness.

The cause for which we stand. The work of Christ is never solo; it is always a choral number, or even better, congregational singing with God's Spirit as song leader. The self is to be perceived and understood as part of a larger whole. In fact it is *from self and sin* that we are to be *made free*. Christ came to form us into faith communities of grace, love, peace, and justice. *Together* is one of the most important words in the Christian's vocabulary.

Yet grains of wheat, before they grow, are buried in the earth below. All that is old doth perish there to form a life both new and fair. The old does keep on dying and the new keeps coming. After crucifixion comes resurrection. The passing of the old makes way for the emergence of the new. In seminaries something is always being buried so new life may spring forth. Yet as we participate in this process we need discernment and wisdom from above to recognize the difference between eternal truth and good, and what is new reality breaking forth to be embraced, internalized, and embodied. God gives us wisdom so conservatives and progressives learn to live together, work together, and allow God to do Christ's new thing.

Through suffering thou, O Christ, didst go, ...and leadest now the selfsame way those true in faith and love. Conflict and suffering come with the territory, but Christ is with those who follow him. Christ, in fact, is our peace (Eph. 2:14). In this enterprise there is no resurrection without a cross, no freedom without discipline, no grace without discipleship, no truth without love, and no peace without what our forebears called *Gelassenheit.* It includes forgiveness rather than retaliation, and doing good instead of doing violence. It means learning to let go and let God retake control.

To the light, eternal light, from darkness into light. Henri Nouwen once observed that it makes all the difference in the world whether one sees the life and death cycle as a movement from light into darkness, or conversely, from darkness into light. How powerfully 1 Peter reminds us that we are called out of darkness into light and that through the resurrection of Jesus Christ we are born into a living hope. While darkness continues its tragic and destructive presence in our world, we know that in following the one who is the light of the world, we too enter eternally into the light of God.

At the center of the bulletin board above my desk are the words "Jesus is Lord," which Winifred painted for me years ago. That was the confession of the early church. It was my confession when I was baptized seventy-three years ago. It is still my confession in shorthand, but with infinitely greater implications than when I first declared my faith. This too is what I am saying when I sing "The work is thine, O Christ." I sing of the coming, the teaching, the living, the suffering, the dying, the resurrection, the exaltation, and the promised coming again of Jesus Christ, which has given focus, direction, and dynamic to my life and ministry, as I perceive it. All praise be to God who was in Christ reconciling us to God and one another, transcending all that threatens to divide us.

In response I praise and thank God with all that is in me. I also thank the many people God has brought into my life so we may love and serve God together. I am more grateful than I can possibly say to all who have participated in the writing, compilation, and publication of this Festschrift, and in any way in this celebration of God's grace through the years. *SOLI DEO GLORIA.*